Awake in the Darkness

Awake in the Darkness

Martin Smith

1

A wake in the Darkness
By Martin E Smith

Dedication

To my mom and dad, my two brothers, and all the friends and family who stood by me through this journey.

And most importantly, to my friends Bob and Mike.

For now, all I can do is endure. To hold on to the slivers of hope and memory, to resist the pull of despair. To believe that even in the darkest night, there is a promise of dawn.

Introduction

Thank you for taking the time to read my story. This book wasn't written with the intention of being a polished or neatly packaged narrative. It began as a means for me to process my thoughts, emotions, and experiences—an outlet to make sense of the chaos that had consumed my life. But as I wrote, I realized that my story might hold value beyond my own understanding. It dawned on me that others might find something in these pages that resonates with them, something that could offer comfort, clarity, or simply the reassurance that they are not alone.

Life can sometimes throw us into situations we never imagined we'd face—situations that test our strength, our sanity, and our very will to keep going. My story is one of those situations. If you or someone you love ever find yourselves in a similar circumstance, my hope is that this book might serve as a guidepost, a flicker of light in the darkness. While I sincerely hope you never have to walk the path I've traveled, I know that life can be unpredictable. And if you do find yourself there, I want you to know that you are not alone.

This book is not a chronological account of events, neatly organized from beginning to end. The order of what happened in these pages does not follow the typical arc of a story that starts with the beginning and concludes with the end. Instead, it's a reflection of my reality as it unfolded, in all its disjointed and fragmented ways. What you're about

2

to read is a raw, unfiltered portrayal of how I experienced those moments, as chaotic and confusing as they were.

When you read this book, I ask that you keep this in mind. Understand that the events and emotions captured here are not presented in a linear fashion, but rather as they came to me, often in waves that threatened to drown me. This is my truth, my experience, and it is far from tidy or coherent. But it is real, and it is mine.

In sharing my story, my hope is that it might offer some insight into what it feels like to be caught in a situation where reality blurs, where the lines between what is and what isn't become nearly impossible to distinguish. If this book helps even one person—whether it's by providing understanding, offering solace, or simply letting them know they are not alone—then it will have served its purpose.

So, as you turn the pages of this book, I ask that you approach it with an open mind and an open heart. Let it be what it is—a journey, a struggle, a search for meaning in the midst of overwhelming uncertainty. This is my story, and I offer it to you in the hope that it might bring some light to the darkness, some peace to the chaos, and some comfort to the pain.

Chapter 1

The Darkness

"Am I dead? Is this my eternity?" It feels like I've awoken in a dark void, an abyss of nothingness. I have no memory of how I got here or where I was before. All I see is an endless expanse of blackness, stretching infinitely in every direction. There is no light, no hint of anything beyond this oppressive darkness.

I grasp at the threads of my memory, but they slip through my fingers like grains of sand. I cannot recall where I was before this disconcerting moment, nor can I remember any past actions or intentions. It feels as though I have abruptly awakened in a dimension where the concepts of time and space have been obliterated—an unending void that surrounds me, saturating the air with an unsettling silence that is both profound and stifling.

I try to move, but my body doesn't respond. I'm paralyzed, trapped in this void. There's no sensation of hot or cold, just an overwhelming numbness. Panic sets in as I realize I can't feel anything at all. My mind races, thoughts jumbled and incoherent.

Fear grips me, a primal terror that claws at my sanity. I am utterly alone, lost in this void. Confusion clouds my thoughts, making it impossible to focus. I am scared, more scared than I've ever been, and I can't shake the feeling that I might be stuck here forever.

At first, the confusion holds sway, a bewildering sensation that keeps me in a state of shock. But as the moments stretch on, an insidious fear begins to crawl into my consciousness. It wraps around me like a thick shroud of dread, constricting and tightening with each passing moment, instilling a sense of urgency and despair.

The darkness envelops me entirely, an impenetrable void that offers no sense of direction or clarity. I find myself suspended in a state of uncertainty, teetering on the precipice of consciousness. Am I awake, or has sleep woven its deceptive threads around my mind? The confusion is palpable, and my surroundings offer no solace or answers. The air is thick with an unsettling stillness, yet faintly I can discern muffled sounds that suggest the presence of other people. Their voices are distant and fragmented, like whispers carried off by the wind, suggesting they might be close yet remain just out of reach in this engulfing darkness.

Questions whirl through my mind with urgency: What is happening to me? Where exactly am I situated? The overwhelming blackness seems to swallow all memories of how I arrived in this state, leaving me in a bewildering void. I reflect on my last clear thoughts, but they are elusive, slipping away like grains of sand between my fingers. Was there a moment before this all-consuming blackness? I struggle to piece together the fragments of my past, but it is as though they dissolve into the air, leaving no trace behind.

My heart pounds in my chest, each beat reverberating in the oppressive silence. I try to move, but my limbs feel heavy, as if weighted down by an unseen force. Panic wells up inside me, threatening to engulf my thoughts. I take a deep breath, attempting to calm myself, and focus on the sounds around me.

The sounds I hear are initially just noise, an indistinct cacophony that I can't describe. They seem familiar, like I should recognize them, but I can't place them. "Why can't I remember?" I wonder, panic rising. The best I can describe are beeps and bells, but even that feels uncertain.

This dark void muffles everything, making it hard to discern what I'm hearing. The sounds are constant, but there's also a louder ringing noise that pierces through the confusion. It's disorienting, and fear grips me as I struggle to make sense of it all. The more I try to focus, the more the sounds blur together, amplifying my terror and confusion.

Through the confusion of all the muffled sounds I am hearing, I detect voices. They are there, but I can't understand anything being said. It's as if I'm hearing a foreign language, something familiar yet completely incomprehensible. The voices are muffled, distorted by the void, but I can hear them. This only adds to my bewilderment and fear, as I struggle to grasp any meaning from the chaos around me.

The voices—yes, they are definitely human—offer a glimmer of hope. Perhaps if I could somehow reach out to them, they might provide the answers I desperately seek. I gather my resolve, mentally preparing to call out for assistance. I part my lips, ready to form the words that might bridge the gap between me and them. However, as I try to speak, the effort reveals an unsettling truth: while I can hear myself within the confines of my mind, there is no sound that escapes into the darkness, no reverberation of my voice that might guide me back to clarity. The weight of silence is profound, and the realization deepens my sense of isolation, leaving me stranded in this profound and haunting obscurity, yearning for connection and understanding.

"What is going on?"

The question reverberates through my mind, a desperate echo that seems to arise from the very depths of my being. Yet, as I search for clarity, no words break through the suffocating blackness that surrounds me. The silence not only muffles my thoughts but also amplifies my uncertainty, leaving me trapped in a paralyzing state of inaction, desperately yearning for understanding in a space devoid of answers

"Is anyone here?" The question hangs in the air, but silence responds with a deafening presence.

"Can anyone hear me?" Again, the only reply is a profound stillness that amplifies the anxiety coiling within.

My thoughts race, quick and chaotic, with the most powerful urging me to surrender, to give into this overwhelming void, relinquishing all hope as I wait for whatever fate has in store. Yet, just beneath that impulse lies a torrent of questions that flood my consciousness:

"How long have I been trapped in this disorienting space?"

"How much longer can I endure this uncertainty?"

The most terrifying question of all hangs unspoken, lingering in the shadowy recesses of my mind: "Is there even a way out?"

In an effort to reclaim some semblance of my former self, I strain to remember anything—faces of loved ones, places that felt like home, moments that contributed to the tapestry of my identity. Yet every attempt to summon these recollections feels like trying to seize smoke with bare hands. My memories evade me, locked away as securely as the world beyond this oppressive darkness. The occasional fragment flits through my mind, but it remains intangible and ephemeral, providing no comfort. Instead, they only deepen the void, creating an even heavier cloak of questions.

Within this nebulous confinement, time itself seems to dissolve. Seconds stretch interminably into what could easily be mistaken for hours or perhaps even days. With no method of measurement or reference point, I find myself adrift in an ocean of shadows. The attempts to gauge the passage of time feel utterly futile; it slips through my grasp as sand through an hourglass. My only reality becomes this overwhelming dark expanse, punctuated sporadically by stabs of pain and the whispers of disembodied voices. Although my body may feel paralyzed, my mind remains a whirlwind of emotions, cycling relentlessly through fear, anger, despair, and a stubborn flicker of hope that refuses to be extinguished.

In this encroaching darkness, the act of looking around in search of signs or anchors in reality is not a viable option. Instead, the necessity to focus on what I can perceive—the sounds that may offer an indication of life, a sense of direction—becomes paramount.

"Is there anything here that can provide me with hope or a sense of latitude in this dire situation?"

An even more pressing question looms, "Will my efforts to listen merely amplify the fear and loneliness that already envelop me?"

These inquiries swirl around me, intertwining with the engulfing silence, echoing in the cavernous recesses of my mind as I confront this harrowing existence. Just as that question crosses my mind, a sound comes from the darkness—a faint, almost imperceptible rustling, like the whisper of leaves in a distant forest. It's so subtle that I wonder if I'm imagining it, a desperate creation of my mind longing for any sign of life.

"Wait!" In the enveloping darkness, my mind is besieged by a torrent of questions, each one more frantic than the last. A heavy blanket of fear presses down upon me, yet I sense the faintest glimmer of something—a voice, perhaps multiple voices, cutting through the obscurity that surrounds my thoughts.

This voice, though barely perceptible, remains resolute in its presence. It weaves through the shadows, murmuring and whispering in a manner that feels oddly familiar. I strain my ears to catch even the faintest snippets of the conversation, fragments of sentences floating toward me like elusive wisps of smoke. Each fragment suggests the existence of a world that lies just beyond my immediate grasp, tantalizingly close yet frustratingly out of reach. A primal need surges within me—the urge to connect and comprehend what is unfolding. As the murmur persists, I am compelled to believe that perhaps someone is seeking me out, calling my name amidst the chaos. I summon the strength to respond, asserting,

"I'm here! Yes, I can hear you!"

But the silence that follows my declaration is deafening, as if my words dissolve into the void without a trace. Panic begins to settle in as uncertainty washes over me like a cold wave.

"What is going on? I am really worried and getting even more scared.

Why don't they hear me?"

The question echoes in my mind, spiraling into a vortex of anxiety. I grapple with the challenge of communicating my awareness, of somehow bridging the gap between me and these elusive voices that surround me.

Straining my senses, I concentrate fully on the sounds enveloping me. The voices, now seemingly omnipresent, surround me in a cocoon of sound. As I focus intently, the whispers grow slightly louder, more distinct, evolving from vague murmurs into something more structured and rhythmic. It dawns on me that this is no random cacophony; rather, it resembles the approach of footsteps, measured and purposeful, drawing nearer with each passing moment.

My heart races, a tumultuous blend of hope mingling with dread. Then, abruptly, silence descends. The stillness stretches on, feeling like an eternity—a stark contrast to the cacophony that had just enveloped me. In this quietude, other sounds emerge, softer yet equally resonant, threadbare echoes that slip through the darkness. It becomes clear that outside of these sporadic voices, I am alone, suspended in this disorienting void.

The silence is oppressive, pressing down on me with an almost physical weight. I try to move, to make any sound that might break through this barrier, but my efforts are futile. The realization that I am trapped in this state, unable to communicate or connect, sends a fresh wave of panic through me. My mind races, searching for any possible way to reach out, to make myself heard.

At this point, I can't distinguish seconds from minutes, or minutes from hours. It's all a blur, and I can only guess. There's no way for me to really know. "Does time even have meaning here?" I wonder, but the question feels less important compared to the others swirling in my mind. "So, for now, I just make the best guess I can," I decide, though the uncertainty gnaws at me, adding to my confusion.

In this dark void, the minutes seem to stretch into hours, each one more agonizing than the last. The isolation is suffocating, and I feel myself teetering on the edge of despair. But amidst the fear and uncertainty, a small spark of determination ignites within me. I refuse to give up, to let this silence consume me. I will find a way to break through, to make my presence known.

With renewed resolve, I focus once more on the sounds around me. I listen for any hint of a response, any sign that my efforts are not in vain. And as I do, I begin to notice subtle changes in the environment—a faint rustling, a distant hum. These small sounds become my lifeline, a reminder that I am not entirely alone in this void.

As I embark on solving this intricate puzzle, I decide to start with the sounds that seem constant. The beeping, the bell sounds, and other noises surround me. It's challenging to remember what certain sounds or things are. I focus on the beeping sounds because they seem to be the most persistent. The talking comes and goes, but I can't understand much of it. So, I intently listen to the beeping, trying to decipher what it could be. "Maybe a clock?" I guess, but then I notice the beeps sometimes speed up and other times slow down. I strain my mind, trying to remember. This sound feels so familiar to me.

Sometimes the beeping stops, and a loud bell goes off, reminding me of an alarm clock. Then I hear light shuffling, as if someone is approaching me, and the bell goes off again, restarting the beeping.

The sound of whatever or whoever came close makes me decide to shift my focus from these sounds to the voices I hear. The rustling, which sounds like people walking, becomes my new clue in this auditory puzzle.

I cling to these fragments of sound, using them to anchor myself in the present. Each one is a thread, connecting me to the world outside, giving me hope that I will eventually find a way to communicate. The journey is far from over, but I am determined to keep fighting, to hold on to the belief that even in the darkest night, there is a promise of dawn.

Chapter 2

Voices in the Void

The voices surrounding me seem to drift in and out of my awareness, creating a haunting ambience that lingers in the obscurity where I find myself. Every utterance, every distant conversation pulls at my consciousness, igniting a desperate urge to respond.

"Please help me! What is happening? Why can't anyone hear me?"

Each plea echoes in the dark, but it appears that my words dissolve into the void, unheard and unanswered. In the depths of this disorienting silence, I contemplate the possibility of following the sounds that envelop me, of tracing the origin of the voices that taunt me with their presence. However, despite my increasing desperation, I find myself firmly anchored to my current spot, as though an invisible force immobilizes me. I search frantically for the source of my confinement, yet there are no visible restraints—no chains or straps to explain my condition. It is simply me, alone in the consuming darkness.

As time stretches on, the darkness becomes a canvas for my fears and anxieties. I begin to question my own existence, wondering if I am merely a figment of my own imagination, trapped in a perpetual state of limbo. The voices, once a source of hope, now seem to mock my helplessness, their indistinct murmurs blending into a cacophony of despair.

I decide at this point to fight. My mind is my only weapon, and I will do whatever it takes to find out where I am and what is happening to me. I decide on working with memories. Past or present, I need to remain calm and try to think. My mind feels blank, but there are flashes of people and places entering my thoughts. They are fast and disorienting, but they are there. My best guess is that these are family, friends, and places I have been or lived. "Could it be that the voices I hear are loved ones?" Or are they sounds from my past? I begin to question once again if I am even alive.

I try to focus on the memories of my life before this void, clinging to the fragments of joy and love that once defined my existence. Faces of loved one's flash before my eyes, their smiles a stark contrast to the bleakness that surrounds me. These memories become my lifeline, a beacon of light in the impenetrable darkness.

Yet, even as I hold on to these precious moments, I am haunted by the uncertainty of my fate. "

Will I ever escape this void?"

"Will I ever be able to communicate with the outside world again?"

The questions swirl in my mind, each one more daunting than the last. They come at me from all directions, a relentless storm of uncertainty. Amidst the turmoil, a small glimmer of hope flickers, fragile but persistent. I refuse to surrender to the darkness, determined to find a way back to the light, no matter how long it takes.

As these questions circle around in my mind, I begin to feel the weight of dread and despair pulling me down, deeper into the abyss. The voices in my head are a constant presence, sometimes seeming to speak directly to me, other times conversing among themselves as if I am not even there. It's a confusing and unsettling experience, making it hard to distinguish reality from the chaos within my mind.

The voices are fragmented, snippets of conversations that make no sense. They overlap, merge, and then split apart again, creating a cacophony that is both familiar and alien. I strain to catch a coherent word or phrase, but it's like grasping at smoke. The more I try to focus, the more elusive they become.

The voices grow louder, more insistent, but still, I can't understand them. It's as if they are speaking in a language, I once knew but have now forgotten. The dissonance is maddening, driving me to the brink of despair. Yet, amidst the chaos, that small glimmer of hope remains, a beacon in the darkness.

I cling to it, determined to fight, to find a way out of this void. My mind is my only weapon, and I will use it to piece together the fragments of my reality. I will not let the darkness consume me. I will find the light, no matter how long it takes.

Just as I start to listen more intently to these voices, trying to make sense of their words and intentions, something unexpected happens. A loud voice, clear and commanding, cuts through the noise. It feels as though someone is standing right next to me, shouting, "MARK, RESPOND!" The suddenness and intensity of the voice jolts me, breaking through the fog of my thoughts and pulling me back to the present moment.

Then a sudden jolt of pain interrupts my thoughts.

"OUCH!"

I exclaim, and amidst the haze, a clear voice pierces through.

"Mark, respond! "

The pain strikes again, relentless and sharp, accompanied by the insistence of that same voice demanding, "Respond."

Each occurrence seems endless, repeating the same cycle. I sense a cruel hand grabbing the right side of my stomach and pinching my skin, seizing it with an agonizing twist.

"PLEASE! Stop, I can't endure this pain,"

I cry out internally, trapped in this looping torment. The pattern emerges; it appears to repeat every hour or two, a cycle of pinching and twisting that stretches on interminably.

I seize the opportunity between the pinching and twisting. That brief respite this woman has given me to think. "She called me Mark?" A spark of recognition flares up. "Yes, that's my nickname! I do remember that now." And then my excitement is interrupted.

"Respond!"

Again, the feeling of someone or something grabbing my skin with a mighty pinch and twist.

"Respond!"

She repeats with the twisting.

"Respond!"

The cycle of pinching and twisting continues after each command.

The command reverberates in my mind, uttered in what I recognize as a woman's voice—yet, her identity remains a puzzle I cannot solve. "Who are you? Why are you doing this to me?" I ponder in desperation, seeking an answer to my plight.

Finally, a fleeting reprieve interrupts what I have come to term my "torture session." An opportunity arises to focus on breaking free, to summon the will to move. I attempt to wiggle my fingers, flex my hands, and shift my feet, but my efforts yield no results—my body remains unresponsive, as if it has been rendered a statue imprisoned in this abyss. I must find a way to move so that when this unknown tormentor returns, I can offer some form of response. Yet, hopelessness begins to settle in; no movement, no change, only a profound sense of entrapment.

"Respond!"

The voice cuts through the silence again, accompanied by a renewed intensity of the agonizing twisting of my skin. I flinch as the pain surges through my right side, a sensation all too familiar. I turn my gaze to the area where the torment seems to originate, but there is nothing to see—no hands inflicting this suffering, merely the excruciating reality of my own pain.

"How is this possible?"

The question reverberates inside my skull, but it feels lost, tangled in the chaos that is me. The pain is not just a sensation; it is everything—my reality, my prison. It surges through every nerve, searing my flesh, flooding my mind. I can barely comprehend where I end and the torment begins. None of this makes sense. I shouldn't be able to feel this much pain, not like this. I shouldn't be able to feel at all.

"How can I respond when I can hardly grasp my own existence?"

The voice cuts through the fog in my head, sharper and more impatient now, like a knife scraping against bone.

"Respond!"

The command slams into me like a physical blow, the demand filling the air with a suffocating weight. The grip on my stomach tightens, twisting my skin to the point of tearing, and the agony becomes a tidal wave, an all-consuming flood that swallows me whole. It's like drowning in fire; I can't breathe, can't think. My own tears sting my eyes and burn down my cheeks, but they seem to evaporate into the void before they can reach my lips. Even my voice is swallowed, snatched away the moment I try to scream.

I'm breaking. I can feel the pieces of myself splintering off, scattered in this darkness. I am stretched so thin I don't know if there's enough left to even call it "me" anymore. The thought sickens me, a heavy, nauseating knot twisting in my gut. I want to fight back, to resist, but what am I fighting? There's nothing, just an endless sea of nothing and the pain.

"She can't hear me."

The words drift through my mind, barely a whisper, and even as I think them, I wonder if I'm speaking to someone else or just to the darkness. I'm not sure which is more terrifying—that I'm alone in this hell or that there's someone there, watching, waiting, and still, I am unheard.

The futility of my attempts weighs heavily on my mind. I am caught in a cycle of pain where each demand for response is met with my silence.

But then, the command rings out again: **"RESPOND!"**

This time, the harsh twist comes as I feel the distinct sensation of tears rolling down my cheeks.

"Am I truly crying?"

The sudden shift in my emotional landscape seems to intercept the onslaught, and the next pinch and twist that I brace for does not arrive. In an unexpected turn, it appears that my tears have spoken for me, finally providing the response that had eluded me for so long. After what feels like an eternity of suffering, the torture has come to an end, leaving me enveloped in a haunting silence that follows the painful ordeal.

The pain coursing through me only leaves me with more questions. "Is this woman a ghost of some kind?" I wonder, the thought creeping in as I strain to make sense of what just happened. There's no one else here, no figure in the darkness, and yet the agony I felt was so real—too real. It lingers like a burning brand, seared into my flesh, and it makes no sense.

Another question gnaws at me, desperate and maddening: "If I'm asleep, why can't I wake up?" The thought slams against my skull again and again, each time more frantic than the last. I don't know if I'm caught in some cruel nightmare or if this is something else, something far worse. But one thing is clear—whatever this place is, I need to escape. I need to find a way out, to understand what's happening, and why. There has to be a way to get answers, a way to claw my way out of this suffocating darkness.

3

Chapter 3

The Struggle to Communicate

In the brief interludes that punctuate the commands and the lingering pain, I find myself focusing intently on the sounds that surround me. The voices that echo through the dim expanse, the faint murmur of conversations just beyond my comprehension, and the subtle shifts in tone that seem to arise from an indistinct multitude. These sounds appear to emanate from all directions, creating a disorienting whirlwind of auditory sensations, yet paradoxically, they feel as though they come from nowhere at all. I cannot discern whether these voices aim to assist me in my plight or if they are merely components of this ongoing torment I endure. The uncertainty of their intentions gnaws at my psyche, but amidst the chaos, it is all I have to cling to as I navigate this harrowing experience.

In the stillness of the darkness, my mind plays tricks on me, especially when enveloped in complete darkness. The faint sound of footsteps approaching can stir a sense of unease, amplifying the silence with each imagined step. It's difficult to determine reality from imagination when your senses are deprived of sight, leaving your hearing to compensate and often overcompensate. Such moments can make the hairs on the back of your neck stand up, creating a heightened sense of alertness. Whether it's a trick of the mind or something real, it's important to stay calm and assess my surroundings cautiously.

But the fear doesn't stop there. The darkness itself seems to pulse with a malevolent energy, as if it is alive and watching me. Shadows twist and writhe at the edges of my vision, forming grotesque shapes that vanish the moment I try to focus on them. The air is thick with an oppressive weight, pressing down on my chest and making it hard to breathe. Every creak of the floorboards, every rustle of fabric, sends a jolt of terror through my body, leaving me paralyzed with dread.

I can feel the presence of something unseen, lurking just out of sight, waiting for the perfect moment to strike. The anticipation is almost worse than the fear itself, a constant, gnawing anxiety that eats away at my sanity. I am trapped in this nightmare, with no escape in sight, and the only thing I can do is endure. To hold on to the slivers of hope and memory, to resist the pull of despair. To believe that even in the darkest night, there is a promise of dawn.

"Is she returning?"

I braced myself for the command and the pain that went with it. Listening as the footsteps draw nearer, they eventually halt abruptly, leading to a silence that envelops me like a heavy shroud. This stillness feels even more deafening than the noise that preceded it, filled with the weight of unspoken anticipation and dread. I hold my breath, keenly aware of the emptiness around me, waiting for any indication of what may come next. Finally, the silence is shattered by a voice—a new voice that is soft yet clear—piercing through the oppressive quiet.

"Mark, can you hear me?" followed by the insistence, "Can you respond to me?"

This voice is distinctly different from that of the cruel woman who has tormented me. It is imbued with a note of concern, perhaps even a glimmer of compassion, that resonates deeply within me. The contrast is stark, igniting a flicker of hope amidst the despair.

I yearn to scream, to reach out and beg for help, but once again, my efforts to articulate my thoughts fail to breach the suffocating darkness that surrounds me. All I can do is cling to the hope that this voice, this person who speaks with such intention, can somehow sense my presence, can recognize my desperate need for rescue.

In an effort to establish a connection, she first asks me to squeeze her hand. As I look down to where my hands should be, I realize with a sinking feeling that there is nothing there. The question reverberates in my mind.

"How can I squeeze a hand that is not there?"

My thoughts momentarily dance around the notion of being a ghost, adrift and disconnected from the physical world. Yet, her voice continues to implore me to squeeze her hand, urging me to respond. With each fervent request, I look down again, searching for this elusive hand, hoping to find some tangible means of interaction, but it remains absent.

Despite my futile attempts, I try to comply, clinging to the belief that someone recognizes I can hear them, that my presence is not entirely lost. My efforts appear inadequate, as she repeatedly asks the same thing, the urgency in her tone rising with each iteration.

Eventually, she shifts her request, moving from "squeeze my hand" to "I am letting my hair down; can you pull my hair?"

In a disorienting moment, I even imagine that she brushes her hair across my face, a fleeting sensation that only heightens my longing for connection.

This woman consistently approaches me with unwavering compassion and concern, her earnest attempts to connect a beacon of warmth in my otherwise bleak existence. Yet, in the depths of my suffering, I find myself grappling with how to respond, feeling trapped in a chasm of silence, where my thoughts and desires remain unvoiced.

Despite the empathetic overtures, I remain at the mercy of my own limitations, unable to bridge the gap between us, hopelessly yearning to convey the depth of my plight.

Out of the suffocating darkness that surrounds me, the deep, resonant sounds of music begin to emerge, reverberating through the air with a powerful intensity that seems to cut through the oppressive silence that has become my constant companion. It's almost as if the music is a lifeline, reaching out to me from the depths of despair and enveloping me in a warm embrace that fills the void I had come to know too well. The notes wrap around me, soft yet insistent, creating a cocoon of sound that drowns out the echoing silence. Almost instantly, I recognize this music; it's familiar, stirring something deep within my memory, as if each chord is a key unlocking forgotten moments of my past.

I focus intently on the distinct voice that resonates from the darkness and the rhythmic pulse of the drums that drive the melody forward. Fragments of recollection flit just beyond my grasp, elusive but tantalizing, teasing me with the promise of clearer memories.

One song follows another in a succession that feels both exhilarating and overwhelming. With each note, I discover a temporary escape from the torment I have endured, a reprieve from the relentless agony that has defined my existence for far too long. The music swells and shifts, transitioning seamlessly from one piece to the next, and I lose myself in the sound, allowing it to wash over me. Then, like a bolt of lightning illuminating a darkened sky, the name of the artist comes rushing back to me—"Rush!"

That realization hits me with a wave of excitement that feels triumphantly alive amidst the chaos swirling around me.

"This is my favorite band," I think, and with that thought, a small flicker of joy ignites within my heart, a feeling so foreign yet so needed in this moment of despair.

As the music continues to play, I notice a mix of songs, predominantly showcasing the unmistakable sounds of Rush, but occasionally interrupted by unfamiliar bands and albums that I struggle to place. Each new melody fills the space, creating a tapestry of sound that engages my senses and challenges my mind. With every pulsating beat, I find myself grappling with the shadows of fear and suffering that threaten to overcome me. For the first time in what feels like an eternity, the darkness surrounding me begins to lose its oppressive quality.

It transforms from a suffocating weight into something less lonely, almost like a quiet companion accompanying me on this auditory journey.

Suddenly, the music shifts again, flooding the space with a voice that grabs hold of me, forcing me to listen. The artist's voice and unmistakable style capture my attention, if only for a moment. But the allure quickly fades as each track unfolds like a fresh stab of reality, I want nothing more than to escape. The album continues, unbroken and unforgiving, each song another nail sealing me in place, and a suffocating dread seeps in. I don't know how I got here, and yet, some part of me fights to understand, scrambling to piece together fractured memories and images that flash across my mind like half-remembered dreams. They taunt me, offering slivers of a past I can't fully grasp.

The album finally reaches its end—only to begin again, starting the entire twisted cycle over, washing over me with that same cruel familiarity. Each note, each verse replays, and an almost visceral recognition strikes me as I identify the artist: Guns N' Roses. I'm hit with fragments of lyrics, each word clawing its way into my consciousness like a bitter reminder of everything I can't escape. The second listen is rough, but the third feels unbearable, and by the fourth, my mind begins to break under the weight of the repetition. It's relentless. I lose track of time, my sense of self eroding with each loop of the same album, over and over, until I'm barely holding onto reality.

The music feels like it's drilling into my skull, the familiarity turning into torture, leaving me raw and frayed. I try to guess how long it's been—eight hours? Twelve? Time is meaningless here; all I know is that I'm trapped in this endless, inescapable loop of sound, each song another wave crashing over me, pulling me under. It's as if someone pressed repeat and then left me to drown in it, the music becoming a cruel prison, an auditory cage tightening around my mind, leaving me alone to endure it.

"Okay, please, someone change this now!"

My thoughts scream silently, a cry for help that remains bottled inside.

"Why am I even asking for aid? No one can hear my anguish!"

Finally, a moment arrives when the music ceases altogether, leaving an unsettling quiet in its wake. The sudden absence of sound feels like a void that swallows me whole, and I reach out desperately for the melody that had become my lifeline amidst the turmoil.

"Please, no more!" I attempt to scream, but my voice echoes in the emptiness, swallowed whole by the silence that envelops me once again.

The stillness is deafening, and with it comes a sinking feeling of despair, a reminder of the isolation I face as I find myself lost in this relentless abyss.

4

C hapter 4
Flickers of Hope

Uncertainty looms before me, casting an ever-present shadow over my existence. As I stand at this precipice, I recognize my lack of foresight into the future that awaits me. Despite this daunting lack of clarity, I persist in my efforts to navigate the complexities and intricacies of this labyrinthine life. I am driven by an instinctive response to the distant murmurs of those around me, fueled by an innate desire to forge connections, to reach out and touch the fabric of shared humanity. However, despite my endeavors, the outcome remains unchanged—no meaningful exchanges occur, and I am left in a state of disillusionment.

In this vast expanse of obscurity, it feels as though I am left to contend with the relentless nature of my solitude. The weight of this isolation presses down on me with a profound intensity, creating an environment that is punctuated by an oppressive silence. This silence, almost tangible in its heaviness, amplifies the intermittent waves of pain that envelop me and wash over me in a ceaseless tide.

Each day, I awaken to the same oppressive silence, a silence that seems to echo the void within me. The isolation is not merely a physical state but a profound emotional and psychological burden that I carry with me. It is a constant companion, a shadow that follows me wherever I go, reminding me of the connections I yearn for but cannot seem to grasp.

Despite the overwhelming sense of desolation, there is a flicker of hope that refuses to be extinguished. It is this hope that keeps me moving forward, even when the path ahead is shrouded in darkness. I hold on to the belief that, somewhere beyond the horizon of my current reality, there lies a possibility of connection, of understanding, and of shared humanity.

In the meantime, I endure. I hold on to the slivers of hope and memory, resisting the pull of despair. I believe that even in the darkest night, there is a promise of dawn. This belief, fragile as it may be, is my anchor in the storm, my guiding light in the darkness. It is what keeps me going, one step at a time, through the labyrinth of life. Each sensation becomes intertwined, blurring together to create a disorienting haze that obscures clarity and fosters an ever-deepening sense of anxiety. The voices that once provided a glimmering thread of hope—those brief moments of connection and understanding—morph into sources of confusion and distress. I find myself grappling with the reality of their existence; are they genuine fragments of the world surrounding me or merely echoes conjured by my troubled mind, illusions woven by the desperation of my circumstance?

The lines distinguishing reality from nightmare continue to blur, casting me adrift in a tumultuous sea of doubt and fear. This relentless cycle of anguish and silence gnaws at my fortitude with each passing moment, compelling me to ponder the nature of my experience. Is this an insurmountable trial, an act of retribution for some misdeed, or simply a threshold separating existence from oblivion? Questions that once carried a sense of urgency now weigh heavily upon my psyche, their answers tantalizingly out of reach, suffocating me beneath their pressing enormity. The darkness that envelops me has evolved over time; it transcends the mere absence of light, transforming into an oppressive force that deeply permeates my thoughts, dulls my spirit, and obscures any semblance of hope that might still flicker within.

Yet, amid the tumult and the shadows, there exists a flicker of belief that refuses to be extinguished. Deep within the recesses of my being, I cling to the notion that this engulfing darkness does not signify an endpoint; rather, it embodies a formidable challenge waiting to be acknowledged and overcome. This belief, a fragile ember amid an all-encompassing night, serves as my lifeline—an anchor that wards off the seductive pull of despair. If the voices I hear possess substance, if those figures that intermittently break the silence are tangible manifestations of reality, then perhaps they hold the key to my escape. They may serve as a lifeline, guiding me back to the world that exists beyond this suffocating void.

In the present moment, my only recourse is to endure this relentless trial. I strive to seize the fleeting threads of hope and memory that still resonate within me, resisting the gravitational pull of despair that seeks to envelop my spirit completely. Even in the depths of the darkest night, I endeavor to maintain faith in the promise of dawn, firmly believing that light will eventually pierce through the oppressive shroud that currently entraps me. I hold on to this belief, for within it lies the potential for renewal and the strength to confront the uncertainties that lay ahead.

With all the despair and gloom pressing in, trying to pull me deeper into the darkness that surrounds me, I suddenly hear voices. "Yes! Those voices... they're my mom and dad," I realize, a glimmer of recognition sparking within me. More often than not, they seem to be talking to each other, their words muffled yet strangely familiar. I try calling out, "I'm here, Mom, Dad—I can hear you!" But my words feel like they're swallowed by the void around me, lost in the darkness.

Then, as if my mom has somehow heard me, I feel a warm hand take mine, a small but comforting presence anchoring me. She whispers something, telling me that Pastor Ice is here again to pray over me. Her voice feels closer, clearer than before, as if she's reaching through the veil separating us. I focus all my energy, trying to make sense of her words. I could be wrong about what I'm hearing, but this is the best I can understand.

I listen as a voice I believe to be Pastor Ice's speaks to my parents for a while before he begins his prayer. His voice is deep and resonant, filled with a power that seems to cut through the darkness itself. As he prays, something astonishing begins to happen—the dense, black void around me feels as if it's lightening, just slightly. "Wait," I think, "Am I imagining this change in the shade? Am I actually beginning to see light?" Hope surges within me, and I cling to it, straining my senses for any confirmation.

When Pastor Ice's prayer comes to an end, I hear my parents, or at least I think it's them, talking softly, saying he has come to see me and pray over me many times. Grateful, I think to myself, "Thank you, Pastor," sending the words out, hoping that somehow, they reach him.

5

C hapter 5
   Moments of Clarity

"That's me, on that bed!"

The thought strikes like a lightning bolt, piercing through layers of confusion and fear with sudden clarity. It's as if I'm seeing myself for the first time, a truth that has always been there, hovering just beyond reach, now suddenly within my grasp. In this instant, something powerful and quiet unfolds within me, a calm realization that sweeps through my mind like a warm breeze dispersing fog. I'm here—whole, aware, and at peace. Floating above myself, I observe with an awe I can't put into words, as if witnessing a miracle that only I was meant to see.

The room is stark and sterile, but I sense a warmth that defies the cold, sterile surroundings—a presence that envelopes the space, filling it with a gentleness unlike anything I've ever felt. This light that surrounds me isn't just light. It feels alive, pulsing with a steady rhythm that mirrors my own heartbeat, sinking deeply into every part of me. It wraps around me, embracing me in an infinite tenderness, like a loving parent holding their child close, whispering without words that everything is all right.

In this light, there's peace—a peace that seems to have been waiting just for me, cradling me like a soft melody that soothes away years of worry and loneliness. I feel whole in a way I didn't know was possible, filled by this love that feels ancient, boundless, and yet intensely personal, as if it was made just for me. It pours into the empty spaces within me, filling them with a warmth that dispels every fear, every doubt. It's a love so complete, so pure, that for the first time, I realize that I was always enough, always loved, and always worthy.

Here, in this stillness, I know peace. It's a peace that tells me I am home.

It feels like being held in the arms of something far greater than myself, a force that radiates love and protection beyond anything words could capture.

As I turn, I find myself in an expansive hallway bathed in the most radiant light, yet it is gentle on my eyes. The light ahead is even more brilliant, but it too is soothing to behold. This light envelops me, guiding me towards a destination filled with peace and protection. The fear and despair that once clung to me in the darkness are now banished, replaced by an overwhelming sense of serenity. I am surrounded by what I can only describe as the profound and boundless love of God. In this moment, I feel an unparalleled sense of comfort and tranquility, as if every worry and sorrow has been lifted from my soul. The light not only illuminates my path but also fills my heart with a deep, abiding peace, assuring me that I am safe and cherished.

I'm moving now, though I don't understand how—there are no steps, no physical effort, just a smooth glide forward. Before me, a long hallway stretches out, but it's unlike any hallway I've ever seen. There are no walls, no ceiling, just endless space filled with floating images, each one a window into the most intimate moments of my life.

"Oh my, that's me..." I breathe, my voice trembling with a mix of awe and sorrow.

The first image that appears is of me as a child, sitting on the big swing set we had in Coronado, California, on the Strand. The scene is so vivid that I can almost feel the cool metal chains in my small hands, hear the rhythmic creak of the swing as I pump my legs, trying to reach the sky.

The salty breeze from the ocean fills my lungs as I gaze out at the Navy exercises on the beach, the sailors moving in perfect synchronization, their figures blurred by the distance. It's a moment of pure, untainted innocence—a memory that had faded into the recesses of my mind, now brought to life with such clarity that it feels as if I'm reliving it.

Tears well up in my eyes as I glide further down this ethereal hall, and more scenes from my life unfold before me. Each image is a precious fragment of my past, a piece of the puzzle that makes up who I am. I see family trips to the beach, the sun casting a golden glow on the waves as they crash against the shore. Laughter echoes in the air, the sound so joyful, so full of life, that it tugs at something deep inside me. These were the moments I had taken for granted, the simple pleasures that now seem so distant, so unattainable.

"Why didn't I appreciate these times more?" The thought stabs at me, a sharp pain that twists in my chest.

I watch myself entering new schools, my young face a mix of nervousness and determination as I walk into unfamiliar hallways. I see the awkwardness of adolescence, the friendships formed and lost, the crushes that made my heart race and then broke it just as quickly. Faces of people who have shaped me—some long forgotten, others still fresh in my mind—flash by, each one stirring emotions I thought I had buried long ago.

Then, I see my family. My mom, her face radiating warmth as she laughs at something one of my little brothers said, the sound of her joy a balm to my weary soul. I see us on spontaneous adventures, driving down dusty roads with the windows rolled down, the wind whipping through our hair as we sing along to songs on the radio.

The love in these moments is so palpable that it overwhelms me, filling me with a bittersweet longing for a time when life was simpler, when I was surrounded by the people I loved most.

My dad appears next, his strong, reassuring presence looming large in the background of so many memories. I see him in the moments before he would deploy, his face etched with both determination and a softness reserved only for his family. He pulls me into a tight embrace, his arms a fortress of safety, and I feel the weight of his love and the burden of his sacrifices in a way I never did before.

"Dad..." The word escapes my lips in a whisper, choked with emotion.

Then, suddenly, I see them—my brothers, Jeff and Andy. They're outside, playing in the yard, their laughter echoing faintly as if from another world. The images shift and flicker, like an old film reel unraveling in my mind. One moment, they're running around, carefree, the sun glinting off their hair; the next, we're all together, playing some game that doesn't even matter.

Then it changes again, to us arguing, shouting over some trivial thing that none of us will even remember an hour later.

The scenes blur and jumble together, the way memories do when they're half-forgotten or just a dream. I reach for them, desperate to hold on, but they slip away like smoke, vanishing back into the light.

Each memory is tinged with both joy and a deep, aching sorrow, as I realize just how precious those moments were and how fleeting.

As I glide further down the hallway, the images start to blur, becoming less distinct, but the emotions they evoke grow stronger, more intense. I am flooded with a tidal wave of feelings—love, regret, joy, pain—all crashing into me at once, leaving me gasping for breath. It's as if the entirety of my life is being played out before me, not just as a series of events, but as a symphony of emotions that swell and crescendo with each passing moment.

Then, I see them—a group of people gathered at the end of the hallway, waiting for me. It's a strange sensation—there's an innate understanding, a deep knowledge of who these people are and what they mean to me, even before I see their faces clearly. My heart swells with recognition, with love so intense that it threatens to break me apart.

There, at the front of the group, stand two elderly couples. I know immediately that they are my ancestors, one pair representing my mom's side of the family, the other my dad's. Their eyes are kind, filled with a wisdom and understanding that transcends time. They smile at me, and the love that pours out from them is so overwhelming that it brings me to my knees.

The couple representing my mom's family says "Please, go back," they say, their voices a harmonious blend of firmness and tenderness that resonates deep within me, like the tolling of a sacred bell.

"It's not your time yet; there is still much more for you to do," the second couple representing my dad adds, their words sinking into my soul, anchoring me to a reality I had almost forgotten.

For a moment, I don't want to leave. The peace, the love, the sense of belonging—it's all so overwhelming, so perfect, that I can't imagine ever letting it go.

It feels like everything I've ever searched for, everything I've ever needed, is right here, in this moment, with these people who have loved me long before I was ever born.

But there's a pull, a gentle yet irresistible force urging me to return. It tugs at me, not with harshness, but with a quiet insistence that I can't ignore. Reluctantly, I turn to go back the way I came, the sense of peace and love still guiding me. I move toward the spot where I first saw my body lying on the bed, the image of it now distant and surreal, as though it belongs to someone else.

Suddenly, I am thrust back into darkness, the same oppressive darkness that had surrounded me before. The contrast is jarring—the light is gone, but its afterglow remains, a faint echo of the love and peace that once filled me. The darkness is familiar, but it's no longer as terrifying as it once was. I'm not afraid, for I know that I am not alone.

The memories of what I endured here flood back—the relentless pinching and twisting of my skin, the endless looping of that one music album, playing over and over for what felt like an eternity, and the sweet yet haunting voice that tried to reach me, to communicate with me in a way that I could barely comprehend. But now, something is different. I have the light's protection, its guidance, and it's leading me toward something—something I can't quite grasp but know I must follow.

Tears well up in my eyes, though I'm not sure if they're physical tears or something deeper, something spiritual. It feels like an expression of my very soul, a response to the overwhelming emotions coursing through me. I focus all my energy on moving, on doing anything to let the voices I hear know that I am still here, that I can hear them.

Time stretches on, each moment feeling like an eternity. But slowly, painfully slowly, I begin to recognize certain voices amidst the darkness.

"Yes! I know that one, that's my mom's voice!"

My heart leaps with recognition, a flood of warmth spreading through me like the first rays of dawn piercing the night.

"Mom...," I whisper, my voice trembling with emotion. Her voice, so soft and comforting, is like a lifeline in this vast sea of darkness.

Then, another voice reaches me,

"Dad!" His voice is strong, reassuring, wrapping around me like a protective shield, grounding me in a way that nothing else can.

"Dad, I hear you!" I try to shout, but the words are trapped within me, echoing only in my mind.

I replay the voices I heard before, trying to connect them with the ones I now recognize. My mom, my dad—I know these voices as well as I know my own.

They are my anchors, the threads that tie me to the world I've almost lost. But there were others too, voices that I can't place, yet they feel important. Were they other family members? Friends? I don't know, but I focus on these voices, using them as a beacon, a guide out of the darkness.

The more I hear my mom and dad, the stronger my will becomes. I cling to their voices, their love, and slowly, ever so slowly, I feel myself moving toward them, fighting my way out of the darkness that surrounds me.

My will grows stronger with every familiar voice that reaches me, each one like a distant star shining through the thick blackness, guiding me toward something I can't yet see. These voices give me hope, a fragile thread to cling to, as I navigate this overwhelming darkness. Yet, in the quiet moments, I can't help but wonder, "Why do I only hear Mom? Why only Dad's voice?" It's a strange, isolating feeling—sometimes it's just one voice, Mom's soft tones or Dad's reassuring words, and other times they blend together, weaving a safety net that holds me steady in the void.

Now that I realize some of these voices are familiar, the darkness doesn't seem quite as lonely as before. It's as though the voices are pushing back the walls of this endless night, creating a small space where I can breathe, where I can remember that I'm still here. But this realization also brings a deep yearning—a desperate need to respond, to reach out to them.

"I just need to find a way to tell them I hear them, to let them know I can hear them, to let them know I am here."

But every time I try, it feels like the darkness tightens its grip, as if it's alive, resisting my attempts to break free.

The more I struggle to force my body into action, the more the despair of this place tries to smother me, dragging me deeper into its cold, endless abyss. The air feels thick, heavy, like the weight of unseen hands pushing down on my chest, squeezing the life from my lungs. I can feel it—this crushing presence—bearing down on me, not just physically but mentally, as if it seeks to break me from the inside out. It's trying to crush my spirit; to snuff out whatever flickering ember of hope still remains.

"No! I won't let it!" I scream inwardly, my voice ricocheting through the silence of my mind. The sound doesn't echo here, as if the darkness absorbs it, refusing to let my defiance spread. Yet, even in the face of this overwhelming force, a fierce determination begins to rise within me, burning like a fire struggling for oxygen in the dead of night.

But somehow, that defiance, that spark of rebellion, doesn't seem to be enough. The darkness pushes back, stronger than I could've ever anticipated, wrapping itself tighter around me like thick chains made of shadow. It's like fighting an ocean current with no shore in sight. No matter how hard I kick, how hard I resist, the tide is pulling me under, deeper into this void that seems to have no end.

"I can't let it beat me," I whisper, the words barely audible, even to myself.

But they are important. They are my tether, my anchor in this sea of blackness. A mantra, a promise, a lifeline that I cling to with desperate hands. I repeat it, again and again, letting it echo through the silence of my soul. It becomes my heartbeat, a rhythm that drives me forward, reminding me that I am still here, that I am still fighting.

And then, as if sensing my defiance, the darkness shifts. It feels alive, aware, as though it has taken notice of me. Everything goes quiet. The whispers, the strange murmurs, the soft hum of voices that I've come to rely on—they vanish, one by one, slipping away like smoke on the wind. An eerie silence settles over me, colder and more suffocating than before. It's as if the entire world has gone to sleep, and I am the only one left awake, floating in this vast, empty space.

The silence is more than a lack of sound. It is a presence in itself, wrapping around me, thick and heavy, making the air feel dense. I've come to guess that this must be nighttime. The familiar voices are gone, replaced by the sterile, mechanical sounds of the outside world. The rhythmic beeping of machines echoes faintly, distant and hollow. Occasionally, a bell chimes, its sharp ring cutting through the quiet, only to fade back into the stillness.

But this quiet feels different now. Less oppressive, perhaps, but still deeply unsettling. It's the kind of silence that feels deliberate, as though the darkness is waiting, watching, biding its time. Suddenly, a new voice cuts through the silence, unfamiliar and unexpected.

"Okay, I'm not sure about this voice."

The thought flickers in my mind, uncertain yet persistent, as I strain to make sense of it. This voice feels different—soft but powerful, carrying a warmth I hadn't realized I'd been missing until now. I listen more intently, trying to catch every word, every subtle inflection, as if this voice holds some hidden truth, something that could pierce through the dense fog surrounding me.

Then, the realization hits me, sharp and sudden: *This voice is praying over me.*

It's like a wave crashing over me, washing away some of the fear and confusion that's been suffocating me for so long. The prayer wraps around me, not in a forceful way, but like a gentle embrace, firm yet comforting, unyielding in its strength. This isn't just a string of words whispered into the void; it's something far more profound. It reaches deep, pulling at the very essence of who I am, tugging at the parts of me that have been buried under layers of despair and darkness.

There's something familiar in the way the prayer carries warmth, reminiscent of the light I had once felt. That light—the one I had thought I lost forever—was a distant memory, and yet here it is again, or something like it. But this time, it feels more tangible, more immediate. The voice is weaving that same protective shield around me, a barrier against the darkness I thought had claimed me entirely. For the first time in what feels like an eternity, the crushing weight on my chest lifts, just a little. I don't feel so alone.

And as if the darkness itself recognizes this change, it starts to pull back. It's hesitant, retreating as if it knows it can't withstand the power of this prayer, this force of love and faith. The oppressive, suffocating despair that had threatened to swallow me whole starts to ebb away, replaced by something softer, quieter: peace. A peace I hadn't thought was possible in a place like this.

The prayer isn't just a shield, though. It's something more. It's guiding me, showing me a path that I couldn't see before. I've been wandering in this endless night for so long, with no direction, no hope. But now, through the voice, I can almost sense a way out, like a map being unfolded before me, one step at a time. I focus harder on the voice, letting it fill every part of me, from the darkest corners of my mind to the deepest parts of my soul.

"Uncle Jesse."

The name slips into my consciousness, and with it, a flood of recognition. Of course. I know this voice. My uncle—his voice has that same strength, that same quiet resolve I remember from when I was a child. He's praying over me, his words wrapping around me like a blanket on a cold night. Somehow, even here, in this place of shadows and silence, he's found me. And his prayer—it's working. It's not just words spoken out of duty or habit. It's alive, pulsing with a warmth that feels almost like light. A warmth I haven't felt in so long.

As he continues to pray, I let the words wash over me, cleansing me, filling every corner of my being with that same warmth and light I thought I had lost. It's as if each word is pushing back the darkness, little by little, replacing it with something new, something I didn't even dare to hope for: hope itself. For the first time in a long while, I feel like I can breathe again.

As soon as I remember my Uncle Jesse's name, a jarring flash of memory hits, leaving me in a whirlwind of confusion. "Uncle Jesse lives in California?" I think, my thoughts colliding. "Does that mean I'm in California?" It starts to feel real for a moment—yes, San Diego. I was stationed there, on 32nd Street Navy Base, on the USS Harry W. Hill, DD986. The familiarity of it grips me, grounding me, but the thought slips through my fingers as quickly as it came. "So... am I still in California?"

The questions swirl, and suddenly, like a lightning strike, it hits me—I came home. I left San Diego. But the thought ricochets, leaving me with even more questions, louder, sharper. "Wait... where am I now?" My mind is screaming, struggling to piece together scattered fragments. If Uncle Jesse is here with me, does that mean he's... wherever I am? But where is that? Or am I imagining all of this?

The darkness around me twists reality, the lines blurring so completely that I can't tell what's real anymore. Every thought feels doubled back on itself, tangled, distorted until the difference between memory and imagination is a line I can't find I can't hold.

"Maybe this is it," I think, daring to let the thought form, fragile but persistent. "Maybe this is the way out."

The idea seems almost impossible, like I'm reaching for something just beyond my grasp. But I can feel it now the way the darkness recoils in the face of this prayer, in the face of my uncle's love, and I dare to believe that maybe, just maybe, I'm not lost after all. Maybe there's still a way through this, still a chance for me to find my way back to the light.

I hold onto the sound of Uncle Jesse's voice, grounding myself in it. It feels like an anchor, keeping me tethered to something real, something beyond the emptiness. And as I focus on it, the cold, suffocating abyss around me seems to shrink. The despair that had once felt infinite is no longer so all-encompassing. There is still darkness, yes, but within it, I can sense something else—an exit, a way forward.

I'm not sure where this will lead, or how long it will take, but for the first time in what feels like forever, I believe that I might actually find my way out.

And with that belief comes a new strength, small but steady. I'm still here. I'm still fighting. And maybe, just maybe, I'm not fighting alone.

The voice continues, steady and unwavering, and I cling to it as though it's a lifeline, the only thing keeping me from sinking back into the void. The prayer grows stronger, and with it, so does my resolve. I can feel the light returning, not the blinding brilliance from before, but a soft, steady glow that seems to emanate from within me. It's as if the prayer is awakening something deep inside me, something that had been buried under layers of fear and despair. I feel a warmth spreading through my chest, down to my fingertips, and for the first time, I can sense my own presence here, in this body that I had almost forgotten.

The darkness is still there, lurking at the edges, but it no longer feels invincible. The voices, the prayer—they have given me strength, a renewed sense of purpose. I can do this. I can find my way back.

"I just need to hold on," I tell myself, the words a promise as much as they are a plea.

The prayer continues, a steady rhythm that I match with my breath, in and out, in and out, letting it guide me as the light once did. With each breath, the darkness seems to recede a little more, until I can almost imagine the world beyond it, the world where I belong.

"I won't give up," I vow, feeling the truth of it settle deep in my bones.

The darkness may have had me in its grasp, but I am not defeated. I will find my way back to the voices I love, to the people who are waiting for me.

And so, I focus on the prayer, on the warmth and love that it brings, and I keep moving forward, one breath at a time, one heartbeat at a time, toward the light that I know is waiting for me at the end of this long, dark night.

6

Chapter 6
    Reflections of the Past

I had just gotten home from the Navy on February 10th, the feeling of returning to civilian life still strange and new. For months, I had been surrounded by the structure and discipline of military life, but now, I was back on familiar ground, in a town where every street corner held memories. Ten days later, on the 20th, I found myself itching to reconnect with my friends, to shake off the feeling of unfamiliarity that had settled over me since returning. I decided to pick up Bob and Mike for a day out, like old times. There was something comforting about the idea of falling back into our usual rhythm, of being around the people who knew me best.

As I drove down the familiar roads of our hometown, the landscape unfolding around us like a well-worn memory, I realized just how much I had missed this—the simple comfort of home. The houses, the trees, the stretch of road I had driven down a thousand times before. Everything looked the same, yet it felt different now, like I was seeing it through fresh eyes. I hadn't fully appreciated how much these ordinary sights and sounds had been a part of me until they had been replaced by military bases, barracks, and the endless horizon of the sea.

Bob was in the front passenger seat, his usual spot, playing DJ with the radio like always. His fingers flew over the dials, searching for the perfect song, cracking jokes with that infectious grin of his. He had this way of turning every moment into something lighthearted and fun, even if it was just a car ride. Before long, he had found a station blasting the latest rock tunes, and our car was filled with music and laughter, the kind of easy joy that only old friends can bring. It felt good—like slipping into a pair of broken-in shoes, familiar and comfortable.

In the back seat was Mike, Bob's older brother. He leaned forward between the front seats, his face animated as he talked about some CD he'd been eyeing in my collection. Mike had always been the one with a passion for music, and even though I hadn't seen him in months, it didn't take long before we were deep in conversation, picking up right where we had left off. The camaraderie between the three of us was immediate, like no time had passed at all. It was like falling into an old routine, one that had been put on pause but never really lost.

Our plan for the day was simple, nothing grand—first, I needed to swing by the unemployment office to sort out some paperwork. Then, we'd head over to visit another one of our friends who had just welcomed a new baby into the world. It wasn't anything we hadn't done a hundred times before: errands, a few laughs, catching up with friends. But after months of rigid schedules and Navy protocols, the idea of spending a laid-back day with Bob and Mike felt like a breath of fresh air.

Before we set off for the day, we decided to make a quick pit stop at my house. As soon as we stepped through the front door, I was hit by a wave of nostalgia. It wasn't just the sight of the familiar rooms, but the small things—the way the after-noon sunlight streamed through the kitchen window, casting long shadows on the floor, the faint scent of coffee lingering from the morning, and the low hum of our old refrigerator that had been in the kitchen since I was a kid. Every little detail felt like a part of my past coming alive again, as if nothing had changed while I was gone.

Bob, always the jokester, flashed his signature mischievous grin as he made a beeline for the fridge, not missing a beat. He swung the door open and, as expected, his eyes lit up at the sight of my mom's stash of Pepsi. She had always kept the fridge well-stocked for when we were hanging around the house, and even though we were grown now, some habits never die.

"Good thing she's working," I thought, laughing to myself as we raided the fridge. We grabbed a few cans of Pepsi and helped ourselves to some BBQ sandwiches that had been simmering in the slow cooker since that morning.

I could picture my mom coming home from work, noticing the missing sodas and sandwiches, and shaking her head, mutter-ing something about "boys being boys" under her breath. It was moments like this, so normal and unremarkable, that made me feel grounded again—like maybe life hadn't changed as much as I thought.

Sitting around the kitchen table, Pepsi cans in hand, we ate our sandwiches in comfortable silence for a while, the only sound the occasional hiss of a soda being opened or the faint rock song still playing in the background. It was one of those moments where you didn't need to say anything to fill the space. Being there, surrounded by the people I cared about, was enough. I realized just how much I had craved this kind of simplicity during my time away.

After we finished eating, I felt a strange sense of peace wash over me. The nerves that had been lingering since I got back, that unsettled feeling of not quite knowing how to fit back into my old life, began to fade. This—being home, being with my friends—felt like the first real step toward finding my footing again.

The rich, smoky aroma filled the kitchen, making our mouths water. My mom was always generous, always making sure there was more than enough food for everyone, but I knew she'd give me an earful if she caught us clearing out her stash. But in that moment, it didn't matter—we were just three friends, back together again, enjoying the simple things that made life good.

The trip to the unemployment office was uneventful, as expected. The waiting room was filled with the dull murmur of conversations, the occasional cough, and the rustling of newspapers. A lot of waiting around, flipping through job listings that all seemed to blur together, none of them sparking even a flicker of interest. The ticking clock on the wall seemed to mock us with its slow, steady rhythm, dragging out the minutes into what felt like hours. Every now and then, one of us would glance at the door, eager to be anywhere but there. We shared a few jokes to pass the time, but our minds were already on the next stop, where something more meaningful awaited us

Finally, we left the sterile, fluorescent-lit office and piled back into the car, the fresh air outside a welcome change from the stuffy interior of the waiting room. The real excitement of the day was waiting for us at our next destination: a visit to our friend's house to meet his newborn baby. As we pulled into his driveway, the anticipation grew. There was a sense of something special in the air, a quiet excitement that settled over us as we approached the door.

The door swung open, and there he was, our friend, grinning from ear to ear, cradling his tiny son in his arms. The sight of him holding that little life made something in my chest swell—a mix of pride and disbelief. This was a new chapter in our lives, one that we hadn't quite imagined when we were younger, but it felt right. We were growing up, but in that moment, surrounded by friends, it felt like we were still those same kids who had each other's backs through everything, just with a few more stories to tell and a little more life behind us.

As we sat there, talking about the future, our voices full of hope and excitement, I realized how much these moments meant to me. This wasn't just another visit; it was a reminder of the bonds that time and distance couldn't break. We were more than friends—we were family, and no matter where life took us, that would never change. Sitting there, surrounded by the people who had shaped my life, I felt a deep sense of gratitude for the past, and an unshakable belief in the future that lay ahead of us. The laughter, the shared memories, the promise of more to come—it all reaffirmed what I had always known: that these were the moments that truly mattered, the ones that would stay with us no matter where we went, or how much time passed.

Around 3:30 in the afternoon on February 20th, we said our goodbyes to our friend and his family. It had been a day filled with laughter and memories, but as the sun began to dip lower in the sky, it was time to head back home. We decided to take the country road, a quieter route that always felt familiar and comforting.

It was the same road my mom and dad lived on, and every time I used the car and got back into town, I'd honk as I passed by their house. It was my little signal to let them know I was back, a habit I'd kept since I first got my license. As soon as I dropped off my friends, I planned to head straight there and catch up with them. The drive down the country road was peaceful, the kind of tranquility you only find in places where the landscape stretches out before you, unhurried and untouched by the rush of city life. The fields on either side were dotted with patches of tall grass and wildflowers, swaying gently in the afternoon breeze. The sun cast a warm, golden hue over everything, bathing the world in a serene glow. Bob and Mike were relaxed, the earlier excitement of the day giving way to a quiet contentment as we made our way home.

As we approached the intersection, the one that always made me a little uneasy, I slowed down. It was an old crossroads, the kind where the roads didn't quite align perfectly. The road I was on sat lower than the one that crossed it, and on the left side, the ground rose sharply, covered in thick grass and stubborn weeds that hadn't been trimmed in who knows how long. It made it nearly impossible to see if any cars were coming from that direction unless you pulled out further than you were comfortable with.

I came to a stop, my foot pressing down on the brake as I leaned forward, trying to get a better view. The sunlight was starting to angle lower, casting long shadows that danced across the road. I hesitated for a moment, my mind racing through the usual routine: check left, check right, check left again. The road seemed clear, but with the high ground and the overgrown weeds blocking my view, I knew I couldn't be entirely sure.

I inched the car forward, just enough to try to see past the obstruction. My heart beat a little faster, that familiar unease creeping in as I decided to go for it. I pressed down on the gas, the car beginning to move forward, and that's when it happened—everything went black. One moment I was crossing the intersection, and the next, I was Awake in the Darkness.

7

Chapter 7
Flashes of Light

The darkness still surrounds me, suffocating and heavy, a thick void that feels as though it stretches on forever, without end or beginning. It's not just the absence of light but a living, breathing entity in itself, pressing in from all sides like the crushing depths of an ocean. The weight of it is unbearable at times, like being buried alive, where every breath becomes a struggle, every heartbeat a reminder of how fragile my existence has become. There's no sense of time here. Minutes, hours, days—none of them matter anymore. It's all just one endless, suffocating night, an abyss that swallows everything, leaving me alone with the overwhelming silence and my own thoughts.

The darkness pulses, a sinister rhythm that matches my own heartbeat, as if it's alive, feeding off my fear and despair. Its presence is constant, wrapping itself around me like a predator waiting to strike. Every inhale is like pulling in cold, damp air, thick with the weight of something unseen, while every exhale feels like a surrender to the void—a small piece of myself slipping away with each breath. There's no escape from it, no way to fight back against something so vast, so consuming.

I can feel it pressing down on me, squeezing the air from my lungs, tightening its grip around my mind. And in this place, where there's nothing but darkness, my thoughts become my only companions. But they're not the comforting kind. They twist and turn, unraveling in ways I never thought possible. Memories that once brought warmth now feel distant, faded like the remnants of a life I barely recognize. Faces blur, voices that should be familiar drift in and out, distorted by the weight of the void around me. I reach for them, trying to hold onto something, anything, but they slip through my fingers like sand.

It's as if I'm losing pieces of myself to this place, fragments of who I used to be crumbling away into the darkness. There's no past here, no future—just an overwhelming present where I'm trapped in this suffocating cocoon of nothingness. My mind spins in circles, grasping at fleeting thoughts, memories, and ideas, but they all seem to spiral downward, pulling me deeper into the void.

And yet, in the midst of this black sea, every so often, I think I see something. A flicker. A faint, fleeting glimpse of light. It's so subtle that at first, I think it's just my imagination, a trick of the mind. But then it happens again—tiny, almost imperceptible flashes at the edges of my vision, like distant stars on a cloudy night. They're so faint, so brief, that I can't be sure if they're real or if my mind is playing cruel tricks on me, trying to create something to hold onto in this endless sea of despair.

I strain to see them, squinting into the void, desperate for any sign that there might be something more than this darkness. They remind me of those shimmering illusions you sometimes see on the hottest summer days, when the air ripples with heat, distorting everything around you, making you question what's real and what's not. That's what these flashes feel like—illusory, fleeting, but just enough to make me hope. Just enough to make me wonder.

"Is this real?" I whisper to myself, my voice barely a breath, swallowed up by the vast emptiness. The question lingers in the air, hanging there without an answer. I don't know anymore. I don't know if these flashes are something real, a genuine break in the relentless darkness, or if they're just a figment of my imagination—my mind's last-ditch effort to create something, anything, to keep me sane.

I've thought I've seen things before, too. Moments when I was sure there was something, someone, just out of reach. But every time I tried to focus, they vanished, leaving me with nothing but the overwhelming blackness. Were those real? Or am I finally losing my grip on reality? My mind races, flipping through fragmented memories, trying to piece together some kind of truth. But here, in this place, everything feels distorted, twisted, as if even my own memories are betraying me.

Maybe that's what this place does—it slowly unravels you, making you question everything you once knew, everything you once believed in. And maybe these flashes of light are just another part of that, another cruel trick to keep me on edge, dangling hope just out of reach. But even knowing that, I can't help but cling to them. Because what else do I have? What else is there but this endless night and the faint, fragile hope that these lights, however fleeting, might mean something?

The more I think about it, the more desperate I become. I start to wonder if maybe these lights are a sign, a signal from somewhere beyond the darkness, telling me there's something more, something waiting for me on the other side. Maybe they're not just figments of my imagination. Maybe they're real. I want to believe they're real.

I focus harder, straining to see them again, to catch another glimpse. My heart races as I wait, breath held, for another flicker. I can feel the tension building, my mind sharpening with anticipation. But nothing comes. Just more darkness, more silence. And in that silence, I feel the despair creeping back in, filling the void left by my fleeting hope.

But I can't let go. I won't let go. I hold onto the memory of those flashes, even if they were only illusions. I hold onto the idea that there's something more than this. Because if I let go of that, if I accept that there's nothing but this suffocating void, then what's left? Nothing but the darkness, stretching on forever. And I can't accept that. I won't.

The flashes are few and far between, faint whispers of light barely strong enough to break the suffocating darkness. Yet each one, no matter how brief, brings a subtle shift, turning the pitch-black void into the barest shade of gray. They're like distant stars in an endless night sky—faint, flickering, and so far, away that it's hard to tell if they're real or just my mind playing tricks on me. But they're there, however fleeting, and their delicate glow offers something I haven't felt in a long time: hope.

For the first time in what feels like eternity, I entertain the possibility that I'm not entirely lost. Maybe these lights aren't illusions. Maybe they're something more—something beyond this empty void. Could they be leading me somewhere? Or are they just the desperate creation of a mind slowly unraveling, trying to convince itself that escape is possible?

The thought terrifies me. What if these flashes of light are nothing more than false hope, illusions conjured by my subconscious in a last-ditch effort to stay sane? What if I'm clinging to nothing? A cold shiver runs down my spine at the idea, and for a moment, I consider giving up. It would be so easy to let the darkness consume me. To stop struggling, to surrender to the void, to let go and drift into the nothingness that's been pressing down on me for so long. Maybe then, the suffocating weight would finally lift, and I'd feel... peace.

But no, I can't let go. Not yet. A flicker of defiance surges within me, pushing against the oppressive force of the void. I *can't* give up—not when there's even the smallest chance that these flashes are real. Maybe they *are* leading me somewhere, to something better, something beyond this abyss. I have no idea where I am or how I ended up here, but I refuse to let this be the end. There's more to this darkness. There *has* to be. I just have to find it.

"I must be doing something right," I whisper, my voice trembling, a fragile thread of belief holding me together.

The words feel hollow, like I'm trying to convince myself of something I don't fully believe, but I say them anyway. Speaking them aloud gives them power, however small. "Everything from memories to people's voices is getting familiar to me." It's a tiny comfort, but I cling to it as though it's a lifeline in this sea of nothingness.

The flashes come and go, each one a brief glimmer that lights up the darkness for just a heartbeat before disappearing again.

They don't last long enough for me to fully understand them, but they're *there*. And that's enough to keep me going. Every time one appears, I reach for it, willing it to stay, to grow brighter, to show me the way out of this endless, oppressive night.

But as I reach for the light, the darkness retaliates. It pushes back harder, surrounding me with a renewed intensity. The air grows colder, heavier, and the weight on my chest becomes almost unbearable. It's as if the darkness knows I'm trying to escape, and it's determined to keep me here, trapped in its suffocating embrace. The more I fight, the stronger it becomes, like a living force intent on breaking me.

Yet even as the darkness tightens its grip, I hold on to the hope those fleeting flashes give me. I don't care if they're illusions or not. They're all I have. And in the heart of this unrelenting void, that small, fragile hope is everything. I focus on it, letting it fill me, pushing back against the despair that threatens to pull me under.

"I won't let it win," I murmur to myself, clenching my fists, my resolve hardening. "I can't."

The darkness presses closer, but I don't back down. I can still feel the flickers of light, even if they're faint, even if they're fleeting. They remind me that somewhere, out there in the vastness, there might be something waiting for me—something better than this endless night. And as long as there's even the smallest chance of finding that something, I'll keep fighting.

Because giving up means letting the darkness win. And that's not an option.

My breath comes in ragged gasps, and my heart pounds in my ears, a frantic rhythm that drowns out everything else.

Still, I keep moving, inching forward through the darkness, following the faint glimmers of light like a moth drawn to a flame. I don't know if I'm making progress or if I'm just wandering in circles, but I can't stop. The darkness whispers to me, its voice soft and insidious, urging me to give in, to let go, to stop fighting. But I ignore it, focusing instead on the flashes of light, on the distant memories that feel like they're slipping through my fingers.

I think of the people I've known, the voices I've heard, the places I've been. They're all so far away now, like echoes from another lifetime. But I hold onto them, refusing to let the darkness take them from me. Each memory is a thread, a connection to the world outside this void, and I weave them together in my mind, creating a fragile tapestry of hope.

Maybe, just maybe, if I can hold onto these memories, if I can keep following the flashes of light, I'll find my way out. Maybe there's something waiting for me beyond this darkness, something worth fighting for. And so, I keep moving, one step at a time, through the endless night, holding onto the faintest glimmers of hope as if my life depends on it. Because, in the end, it does.

I cling to the belief that these flickers of light mean progress. It's all I have right now. I exhaust myself trying to make sense of the voices I hear, straining to identify them, to connect them to faces from my past. It's like trying to piece together a puzzle in the dark, where the edges are frayed, and the pieces are worn. When the music plays, I focus intently, trying to name the artist, the songs—anything to keep my mind from slipping further into the darkness.

At this point, I think someone might be putting headphones on my head, a sensation that feels both foreign and familiar, like a memory from another life. The music isolates me further, cutting off the faint, comforting sounds of the voices I've started to recognize, but it also grounds me in a strange way. It gives me something to hold onto, something to focus on in the midst of this endless night. I concentrate on the notes, the rhythm, the lyrics, trying to pull myself out of the fog that clouds my mind.

"Rush!" I suddenly exclaim, the recognition hitting me like a bolt of lightning. My voice echoes in the oppressive silence, reverberating through the darkness. It's as if the very sound of the name has power, a force that begins to unravel the suffocating void around me. The memories are starting to flood back now, one by one, breaking through the barriers that the darkness has erected around my mind.

I grasp at the fragments of my past, and slowly, they begin to coalesce into something tangible.

"2112,"

I whisper, the name of the album bursting into my consciousness like a flare in the night. I can almost hear the opening strains of the overture, the sound swelling, filling the emptiness around me.

"And the meek shall inherit the earth," the words from 2112 echo in my mind, a defiant cry against the void, a reminder of a story where hope and rebellion intertwine against an overwhelming force.

It's a small victory, a single spark of light in the vast darkness, but in this place, it feels monumental, like a lifeline thrown to a drowning man. As the album plays in my head, each track becomes a beacon, guiding me through the shadows.

"We are the Priests of the Temples of Syrinx," I murmur, the lyrics pulsing with a rhythm that syncs with my heartbeat. The stern voices of the Priests seem to mock the darkness, their authority a stark contrast to the chaos that surrounds me.

The song shifts, and I hear the yearning in "Discovery," where the protagonist finds a guitar, a relic from the past, and the music it produces is like a revelation. "What can this strange device be?" the line echoes, the words conjuring images of a time when discovery was still possible, when the world wasn't swallowed by this endless night.

As I mentally play through the album, the music becomes a weapon, slicing through the despair that clings to me. The "Presentation" starts to build in my mind, the protagonist's bold declaration to the Priests that music could change the world.

"Listen to my music, and hear what it can do,"

I can hear the melody clear as day, defiant against the silence that surrounds me.

The "Oracle: The Dream"

rushes through me, and I feel the weight of the ominous prophecy it contains.

"I see the future of the earth is burning," the words hang in the air, heavy with foreboding, yet there is a strange comfort in their familiarity. This prophecy, dark as it may be, is a part of me, a piece of my identity in a world where everything else has been stripped away.

Finally, the epic "Grand Finale" surges forth, its triumphant, yet chaotic notes resonating within me. "Attention all Planets of the Solar Federation,"

I repeat the command, feeling a strange kinship with the doomed protagonist, as if I too am resisting a force much greater than myself. The music fades, but the resolve it has ignited within me remains.

Time stands still for me because I can remember lyrics and names of songs. For a brief moment, the darkness seems to recede, its suffocating grasp loosening as the memories of 2112 bolster my spirit. The familiar notes and lyrics echo in my mind, reminding me of a world beyond this void, a world where I still belong.

In this fleeting clarity, I realize that even in this bleak abyss, I still possess something the darkness cannot take from me—my music, my memories, and, most importantly, my will to resist. They are my lifeline, pulling me back from the edge, giving me the strength to push against the encroaching void.

With the memories of being at that stop sign and the fragments of voices surrounding me, I know something happened. I can feel it in my bones, in the way the memories swirl around me, just out of reach. I just don't know what it is yet. But when I finally find my way out of this darkness, I'll find out what happened. Most importantly, I need to know where my friends are. The thought of them, of their faces, their voices, keeps me anchored, keeps me fighting.

The weight of everything I'm dealing with in this dark world is starting to drag me down again, heavier than ever. The isolation gnaws at me, it's cold teeth sinking deeper into my thoughts, and the uncertainty of it all—it's maddening. I feel like I'm drowning in an invisible tide that rises higher each moment, pulling me under with every breath I take. Each second, each minute, feels stretched, twisted into something more sinister. I try to fight it, to claw my way back up, but the weight presses harder, as if the very air around me is thickening, making it impossible to breathe. Alone in this place, the feeling of hopelessness consumes me, growing like a shadow, stretching far and wide.

I call out, or at least I think I do, but no one answers. It's as if my voice has been swallowed by the darkness, absorbed by the void before it can even leave my lips. I scream, the sound echoing in my mind, but the world around me remains silent, eerily still. It's terrifying, this feeling of being completely disconnected. I know I'm trying to reach out—people are out there; I can feel it. I can sense their presence, like faint whispers brushing against the edges of my consciousness. They're begging me to respond, pleading for me to break through this barrier that separates us, but I can't. My voice is trapped, strangled by the oppressive grip of the darkness.

Confusion twists through my mind, a knot of fear tightening in my chest. Why can't they hear me? Why does the darkness steal every attempt I make to connect, leaving me mute and helpless? The more I try, the more frantic my efforts become, but nothing changes. My words are swallowed before they can even form, and I am left flailing in silence. What's wrong with me?

I feel myself slipping further, sinking deeper into the blackness that surrounds me. It's like a bottomless pit, and no matter how hard I fight, the edges keep crumbling beneath me. I can't stop the fall. Doubt claws at my mind, its icy fingers dragging me down, wrapping tightly around me like a vice.

"Is there a way out?" I wonder, my thoughts spiraling. Panic creeps in, cold and suffocating, as if it's seeping into my very bones. "Am I trapped here forever?"

The fear begins to suffocate me, its grip tightening around my heart until I can hardly breathe. My chest feels heavy, my thoughts chaotic. What if this is it? What if I never escape this void? What if I'm destined to remain here, lost in the dark, while life outside carries on without me?

"Why can't I reach those who are begging me to respond?" My mind races, desperately searching for answers that refuse to come. The frustration bubbles up inside me, boiling over into helplessness. Why is this happening? Why can't I just speak? Why can't I make them hear me?

These questions tear at my sanity, one after another, overwhelming me with their intensity. They grow louder, fiercer, until they drown out everything else. It's all I can hear—these relentless voices of doubt, fear, and confusion, screaming at me, threatening to drag me down even further. They pull me under like an undertow, threatening to bury me beneath the weight of my own mind, where there is no light, no hope, just endless, crushing darkness.

Just when I feel like I'm about to be swallowed whole, when I'm sure I won't make it back from the abyss, I sense something. A faint, barely perceptible warmth against the cold. At first, I think it's a trick, a cruel illusion, but then I feel it again—stronger this time. It's the light. The same calming, peaceful light I've felt before. It pushes through the darkness, soft but steady, like a hand reaching out to me, offering me a lifeline in this endless night.

The light wraps itself around me like a protective blanket, its warmth sinking into my bones. It's comforting, like a mother's embrace, soothing the fear that's been gnawing at me, chasing away the chill of despair. It's as if the light is whispering to me, telling me that I'm not alone, that I haven't been forgotten. There's something—or someone—out there watching over me. The realization hits me like a breath of fresh air. I'm not abandoned.

The fear and confusion don't vanish entirely, but they're quieter now, muffled by the presence of this light. Its warmth gives me the strength to keep going, to keep pushing against the darkness. It's a reminder that, no matter how deep the void feels, there's still something beyond it. There's still a way out, and as long as I can feel the light, I know I have to keep fighting to find it.

Hope, fragile and flickering like the light itself, takes root in my chest, and I cling to it with everything I have. I'm not lost. Not yet. As long as there's a spark, I won't let the darkness win.

By this point, I've felt this light several times, and each time it comes, it brings a sense of peace that I can't quite describe. It's like a beacon in the storm, a guiding star that helps me navigate through the darkness. It envelops me in a way that makes me believe it's more than just light— it's the love of God surrounding and comforting me, much like armor around a knight, shielding me from the despair that threatens to consume me. It gives me the strength to keep going, to keep fighting, even when everything else seems lost. As is in Ephesians 6:10-17 New International Version.

The Armor of God

10 Finally, be strong in the Lord and in his mighty power. 11 Put on the full armor of God, so that you can take your stand against the devil's schemes. 12 For our struggle is not against flesh and blood, but against the rulers, against the authorities, against the powers of this dark world and against the spiritual forces of evil in the heavenly realms. 13 Therefore put on the full armor of God, so that when the day of evil comes, you may be able to stand your ground, and after you have done everything, to stand. 14 Stand firm then, with the belt of truth buckled around your waist, with the breastplate of righteousness in place, 15 and with your feet fitted with the readiness that comes from the gospel of peace. 16 In addition to all this, take up the shield of faith, with which you can extinguish all the flaming arrows of the evil one. 17 Take the helmet of salvation and the sword of the Spirit, which is the word of God.

In these moments, I hold onto the belief that I'm not alone, that there's a force greater than myself guiding me through this darkness, helping me find the strength to keep going. It's this belief, this faith, that keeps me from giving up, from surrendering to the void. It's what gives me hope that, no matter how dark it gets, there will always be light, no matter how small, to guide me through.

8

Chapter 8
Awakening

Again, I see light—but this time, it's not the gentle, peaceful light that once cradled me in its warm embrace. No, this light is altogether different, unsettling, as if it's probing at the very edges of my soul, stirring something deep inside me that I've long buried. The darkness that has suffocated me for what feels like an eternity begins to shift. But it's not a graceful transition, no—it's reluctant, almost defiant. The void that has held me in its cold, unyielding arms refuses to let go, fighting the change with every ounce of strength it has. The blackness that has been my only companion slowly morphs into a murky, oppressive gray, a shade that doesn't feel like a reprieve but rather a warning—a harbinger of something unknown, something I'm not sure I'm ready to face.

And then, out of nowhere, tiny pinholes of light begin to puncture the gray. They appear at random, like stars breaking through a storm-laden sky. But these aren't stars. There's no comfort in them, no distant hope shining down from the heavens. Instead, they are fleeting, appearing for only a heartbeat before being swallowed up again by the dense grayness that surrounds me. Their brief existence makes me question if they were ever real to begin with, or if my mind, desperate for a way out, has conjured them from nothing.

Yet with each flicker, these lights grow bolder, more insistent. As if fueled by their own defiance, they refuse to be extinguished. They expand, like cracks in a dam that's on the verge of breaking, the pressure mounting with every passing second. The light intensifies with every breath I take, growing brighter, more invasive, pushing against the darkness with a force that feels almost violent. It's a battle, and the light is winning—but it's a battle fought with teeth and claws, with a ferocity that frightens me. This light, though—it's not the gentle, welcoming light I once hoped for. It's sharp, blinding, almost painful in its intensity.

I can't decide if this light is a beacon of hope, something that will guide me out of the abyss, or if it's a force far more dangerous, something that will consume me entirely. The more it spreads, the more it devours, swallowing up the darkness that has been my shelter, my prison, my everything. It's terrifying to watch. I had grown accustomed to the dark. In some strange, twisted way, it had become my reality, my normal. Now, as the light overtakes it, I wonder—will there be anything left of me once it's done?

The darkness that once surrounded me, that kept me isolated and alone, is now almost entirely gone. It has been replaced by this harsh, unrelenting light, so overwhelming that I can barely comprehend it. The air feels different—no longer thick and heavy but almost electrified, crackling with energy. The sounds around me, once muffled and distant, now come rushing back with startling clarity, sharp and unavoidable. They slam into me all at once—voices, machines, the world of the living flooding back into my consciousness like a dam has burst open.

I recognize these sounds. I had forgotten them, buried them deep within the recesses of my mind. The steady beeps of machines, the faint murmur of conversation in the background, voices too distant to make out clearly but unmistakably real. And then, louder, closer, a soft, caring voice speaks, cutting through the fog that still clings to the edges of my awareness.

"Can you hear me?" The voice is gentle, but firm, pulling me toward it.

"I'm Nurse Amy," she says, her tone warm, familiar, as though we've met before.

But how? When? My mind spins with confusion, disoriented by the sudden onslaught of sensations. The light, the sounds, her voice—it's too much, all at once, and I don't know how to make sense of it.

I try to respond, to say something, anything, but my voice—like in the dark—won't come. My mouth feels dry, my throat constricted, as if the words are stuck somewhere deep inside me, just out of reach. Panic starts to creep in.

Why can't I speak? Why can't I respond? The fear that had momentarily subsided is back, twisting in my chest, threatening to suffocate me once more.

"Take your time," Nurse Amy says, her voice soothing, as if she knows the battle I'm fighting inside.

"You've been through a lot. Just try to relax. We're here with you."

Her words, though kind, barely penetrate the whirlwind of thoughts and emotions swirling in my head. **Where am I? How**

did I get here? The questions race through my mind, each one more frantic than the last.

As the light continues to grow, as the voices become more insistent, the sense of being caught between two worlds overwhelms me. Part of me clings to the darkness, that strange, cold comfort that had been my constant companion, while another part of me aches to reach out to the light, to the people, to the world beyond this liminal space I'm trapped in. But I'm afraid. I'm terrified of what lies beyond, of what awaits me in the light.

Will I find answers, or just more confusion? Will I be welcomed back, or will I discover that too much has changed? That **I** have changed beyond recognition?

The light presses in on me from all sides, insistent, unrelenting, and I know that soon, I will have to make a choice. I can't stay in this in-between place forever. But even as the decision looms, the fear continues to hold me in its grip, and I find myself paralyzed, torn between the safety of the unknown and the terror of facing whatever comes next.

And in that moment, suspended between fear and hope, the only thing I can do is wait.

It's the same voice that comforted me in the darkness, that kept me anchored when everything else was slipping away.

"Can you hear me? Can you respond to me?"

I try. I try with everything I have, but my words—my voice—it's lost, trapped somewhere deep inside me. All I can manage are thoughts, loud, desperate thoughts that echo in my head but never make it to my lips.

Then I hear them—my mom and dad. Their voices, filled with a mix of relief and worry, explain what has happened.

"A car accident," they say.

"We're in St. Louis," they say.

They talk about my injuries, but my mind can't focus on that. All I can think about is that day, that awful, terrible day at the stop sign.

"Tell me about Bob and Mike," I ask, my thoughts screaming the question, but no one answers. The silence that follows is more deafening than anything I've ever heard. Another voice joins in, the voice of a doctor explaining my injuries, listing them off like a grocery list. But I don't care. I don't care about me. "I don't care about me! ARE MY FRIENDS, OKAY?"

I want to shout, but still, there is no response. I realize, with a sickening sense of dread, that no one can hear me.

"Why won't they tell me?"

I ask myself over and over, each time more frantic, more desperate.

And then, like a freight train crashing into me, the horrible thought hits.

"I killed my friends! This is all my fault!"

The guilt, the shame, the unbearable weight of that thought crushes me. It drains every last ounce of resolve I had left, leaving me empty, hollow. I decide, in that moment, that I should give up, that I should stop fighting. The pain of not knowing, of fearing the worst, is too much. It's too much to bear.

I shut down. I refuse to listen to anyone, refuse to acknowledge anything. My injuries, my situation—it all becomes meaningless in the face of this overwhelming guilt.

"There's no reason to try; it's all my fault!" I tell myself over and over.

"Ask me all you want, but even if I can, I won't respond!"

I close my eyes, wishing for the darkness to return, to take me back, because even that suffocating void is better than the overwhelming, all-consuming feelings that have taken over me.

I hear the nurses, my family, begging me to respond, but I ignore them. It feels like I've been ignoring them for days, no longer trying as I did when I was lost in the darkness.

And then, one day, something changes. Without even trying, my eyes open, as if they've made the decision for me. The light, once so harsh and unbearable, seems softer now, more manageable. As my eyes focus, I see something above me—a poster. It's taped to the ceiling, directly above my head. A poster of Rush, the band whose music helped me reconnect with life as I started to remember. Seeing it, something stirs inside me, something I haven't felt in what seems like forever: joy.

Beside me, I hear a voice, my Aunt Carla's voice, and she says, "Mark went all over St. Louis looking for this poster for you."

Then I hear him—Mark.

"I told them that whether they liked it or not, I was putting it above your head so you could see it when you woke up." His voice is filled with that familiar, stubborn determination, and I hear a couple of laughs at his comment.

And just like that, something shifts inside me. The guilt, the pain, the overwhelming sense of loss—it's still there, but now, there's something else. There's a spark, a tiny, flickering spark of hope.

Chapter 9
Road to recovery

I lay there, unable to move, staring blankly at the Rush poster tacked above my head. The vibrant colors and familiar image felt surreal, almost like a relic from another life—a life that felt impossibly distant now. My mind, once buzzing with activity, was now a murky haze of confusion and dread. The constant whirl of thoughts and fears, everything I'd overheard from the nurses and doctors, started to solidify, turning my nightmares into reality.

But the dread—the relentless, suffocating dread—was the worst. It gnawed at me, sinking deeper into my bones with each passing moment. No one would tell me what happened to my friends. Their silence was a heavy, oppressive thing, pressing down on my chest until I thought I might suffocate under its weight.

"If they would just tell me they're okay, I'd listen, I'd cooperate," I kept thinking, over and over, as if repeating it enough times might somehow make it true.

But they wouldn't tell me. And because of that, I refused to give them anything. I moved my eyes around, trying to get a sense of my surroundings, trying to find something—anything—that would make this nightmare make sense. I must have been noticed because the next thing I knew, the nurses and doctors were swarming around me again, their voices a cacophony of urgent pleas for me to respond.

"Nope. Not going to happen." I withdrew, pulling myself deeper into the safety of silence, where their words couldn't reach me.

One day, a nurse mentioned something about putting a valve on my neck so I could talk.

"A valve? What do I need a valve for?"

The thought terrified me—another piece of this nightmare puzzle that didn't fit, didn't make sense. But when they finally placed the valve, and I felt the roughness of my own voice scratching its way up from my throat, it was like a small victory.

I can hear Nurse Amy and another voice just outside my room, talking softly, as if I can't hear them or won't understand. But I catch bits and pieces—she mentions a "valve" and something about how it'll let me speak. My heart stirs, just slightly. It's been so long since I've been able to say anything, let alone ask the one thing I need to know.

She comes closer, finally in view, holding a small plastic valve. Her expression is cautious, kind, but tinged with a bit of hesitation as she explains, "This will let you talk, but you might sound a little different than you're used to. And... it might be difficult at first. You may not be able to say much."

Different? My voice might be different? But that's not what matters. All that matters is that I'll be able to speak. I nod, barely, just enough to show I'm ready. Amy adjusts the valve, moving slowly, carefully, as if the slightest wrong movement might hurt me. She fits it over my trach, then steps back, her eyes gentle but expectant.

"Try saying something," she says, her voice encouraging.

The words rise up like they've been waiting all this time just for this moment, just for the chance to be heard. I open my mouth, and the question tumbles out, raw, full of hope I can't hide. "How are my friends?"

The room holds its breath, Amy's gaze fixed on me. But she says nothing. I study her face, waiting for a flicker, a nod, anything. But there's nothing—no response, not even the smallest sign that they're okay.

A cold ache starts to spread in my chest. I swallow hard and try again, my voice barely holding itself together. "How are Bob and Mike?" This time, it's almost a plea. Still, silence.

Amy doesn't look away, but her face remains painfully neutral, her eyes not giving anything away. The silence feels like a heavy weight pressing on me, crushing my hopes, piece by piece. She doesn't need to say a thing; her silence answers me more than words ever could. It's as if everything I've feared is suddenly real, each unspoken word hitting harder than the last.

My heart feels hollow. I feel myself drawing back, shrinking inward, trying to escape the pain blooming inside me. If no one will tell me what happened, then I don't want to know. I don't want to think, or feel, or even speak anymore. I let the question fall away, swallowed up by the growing numbness in my chest.

I turn away from her, my gaze drifting up to the poster hanging above my bed—a small, familiar piece of my world in this strange, clinical place. I focus on it, letting it take over, blurring everything else around me.

Over the next few days, Nurse Amy tries to get through to me. She comes in with the same warm look on her face, gently reminding me of the people who care for me. "Can you squeeze my fingers?" she asks, holding her hand close to mine. I don't respond, not even a twitch. Every ounce of my energy is spent on shutting everything out, walling myself off.

She puts the valve on again, urging me softly, "Can you talk to me? Just say something."

I turn my head, the words fighting to get out, despite my better judgment. "How are Bob and Mike?" My voice trembles, edges of desperation slipping through. She still doesn't respond, and something inside me crumbles completely. The silence is louder, harsher than anything she could say.

I close my eyes, sinking back into the only place that feels safe—the familiar darkness that once scared me, but now feels like the only thing I can trust. I let myself drift back there, holding onto the emptiness like a lifeline, wishing I could disappear into it forever.

Everyone keeps trying—Nurse Amy, the doctors, even my parents, who come and sit by my bed, whispering words I can barely bring myself to hear. But I'm done. I don't respond; I don't look at them. I don't want their comfort. I don't want their words. I just want to be alone, back in that void where nothing can reach me, where nothing can hurt me.

Then, out of nowhere, a voice sliced through the noise—a voice I knew, one that instantly pulled me back from the edge.

"Hey? How ya doing, bro?" It was like a lifeline, and before I could even register what was happening, his face came into view.

"Bob!"

The name burst out of me, a mix of disbelief and desperate hope.

He grinned down at me, his familiar smile bringing a flood of memories, of times when life was simpler, easier. He leaned in close, his face so near that I could see every line, every detail.

"I'm not gonna kiss ya! I'm not gonna kiss ya!" he repeated, laughing, his voice a welcome reprieve from the dark thoughts swirling in my mind.

For a moment, the heavy fog of dread lifted, and I almost laughed with him. But then he grew serious, his tone softening.

"Me and Mike are okay," he said, each word like a balm to my soul.

"Mike's still in the hospital, but he's gonna be fine." The relief was so overwhelming that it felt like I was drowning in it. The tears I'd been holding back for so long finally broke free, and I cried silently, tears slipping down my face as the weight of uncertainty eased just a little.

They were alive. My friends were alive. That was all I needed to know. Suddenly, the endless, dark tunnel I'd been trapped in didn't seem so hopeless.

I was ready to do whatever it took to get out of this place, to get back home, back to some semblance of normalcy. The guilt, the pain, the overwhelming sense of responsibility for their injuries—it would never leave me. But at least I didn't have to bear the crushing burden of knowing they hadn't made it.

Yet, as the relief settled in, new fears began to creep in, insidious and sharp.

"Why am I strapped down? Why can't I talk?"

The questions bubbled up inside me, a rising tide of panic that threatened to pull me under. I tried to speak, to move, but nothing happened. My body, once strong and reliable, felt like a foreign object—a cage that held me prisoner.

Every day, it seemed like a different doctor came to examine me, their faces blending into a blur of detached professionalism. They poked and prodded, murmured to each other in low voices that I couldn't quite make out, and then left me alone with my fear.

The first thing I did was talk to the nurses, then to my dad. When I heard his voice, calm and steady, something inside me started to heal, just a little.

"Do you want to call Mom and tell her?" he asked, his voice gentle but strained, like he was holding back a flood of emotions.

"Where is she?" I managed to rasp out.

"We've been taking turns being here," he explained, his voice softening with each word. "She's at home, finishing her bus route for today."

The thought of my mom, out there in the world, doing something so normal, so mundane, was grounding. "Yes, let's call her!" I exclaimed, desperate to hear her voice, to feel that connection.

When I finally spoke to my mom, the words that tumbled out weren't questions about what had happened, about why I was here, or why I couldn't remember anything. No, instead, I asked for something simple, something normal.

"I want a McDonald's hamburger," I told her, my voice small, almost childlike.

She laughed, and it was like music, a bright, warm sound that chased away some of the lingering shadows.

"I'll bring you one when I come," she promised.

That hamburger became my lifeline, something to cling to in the storm of confusion and fear. It was a piece of the world I understood, a world where things made sense.

When my mom and brothers finally arrived, she unwrapped it for me, and the smell hit me like a wave of nostalgia, bringing back memories of better days. I didn't wait—I tore into it, desperate for that familiar taste, that small comfort. But then, suddenly, I heard Jeff's voice, sharp and panicked.

"Mom! He's going to choke!" he yelled, his voice slicing through the moment of peace.

In my desperation, I had forgotten about the valve, forgotten everything except the need to eat, to feel something real and tangible. They told me I was supposed to take the valve off first, but I hadn't cared. I had been too hungry, too eager to reclaim a small part of myself that I had lost.

"Why are my legs and arms all strapped down?" I asked, the question slipping out before I could stop it.

Mom's face softened, her eyes filling with a sadness that made my chest tighten. "Because you have a broken neck," she explained gently.

"And you kept trying to get out of bed when they first brought you in."

Her words hit me like a punch to the gut, and I struggled to process what she was saying. She continued, her voice trembling slightly.

"When you first came in, we were in the waiting room with your grandma. The doctors were telling us that because of your broken neck, you'd probably be paralyzed." She paused, her eyes brimming with tears she refused to let fall.

"But then your Uncle Richard came in the room and said,

'He's not paralyzed, his legs are kicking all over the place, and he's trying to get out of bed.'"

The weight of her words settled over me like a suffocating blanket, each sentence sinking deeper, pulling me down. They'd already told me about my injuries multiple times, but I hadn't really listened. I hadn't wanted to. But now, I had no choice. I forced myself to hear them, to really understand.

"You broke your neck in three places."

"You had a serious head injury."

"You had a torn aorta."

"Your stomach was in your rib cage."

"Broken ribs."

"Shattered pelvic bone."

Each sentence was like a hammer blow, driving the reality of my situation deeper into my consciousness. And then came the final, devastating blow:

"The doctors say you'll never walk again, never speak correctly, never have kids, and probably never have full use of your hands and arms."

The world seemed to tilt, and I felt myself drifting away, my mind recoiling from the harshness of the truth. The words blurred together, becoming meaningless as I fixated on one thing: never have kids. It was too much. Too much to handle, too much to process.

My mind shut down, retreating to a place where the pain couldn't reach me. I decided then that I would take it one step at a time. First, I needed to get out of this hospital. The rest—whatever that looked like—I would deal with later.

The days passed in a blur of therapy sessions, where physical and vocational therapists came to push my limits, urging me to move, to fight, to survive. Each session was grueling, the pain nearly unbearable, but I forced myself to keep going. I had to. I needed to get out of this place, needed to go home.

One day, Nurse Amy came to sit me up in a bed that doubled as a chair. She wheeled me in front of a large window that overlooked the city, the snow-covered landscape stretching out as far as I could see.

The sight of the snow made my stomach twist in knots, and I felt a wave of irrational anger surge through me.

"Nurse Amy!" I shouted, my voice raw with emotion.

"Patient Mark! "She would yell back at me.

"Get me out of this chair!" I hated the snow, hated the cold, lifeless expanse outside the window. It felt like a reflection of the emptiness inside me, and I couldn't stand it.

She tried to reassure me, telling me it was good to be up and moving, but I couldn't hear her. All I could think about was the pain radiating from my shattered pelvis, the constant, relentless ache that seemed to be getting worse.

"Please," I begged, my voice breaking. "Please, get me away from here."

"Nurse Amy!" I shout, my voice cutting through the quiet of the room. The pain is unbearable; it's like knives digging into my hips and lower back, but she's not here yet. I shift slightly, trying to ease the pressure, but it only makes things worse. The chair I'm strapped into feels like a medieval torture device. Every second ticks by slowly, stretching time with each throb of pain.

"Nurse Amy!" I call out again, louder this time, a hint of desperation creeping into my voice. I hear footsteps in the hallway, and soon she appears at the door, her face calm and composed as always. "Patient Mark!" she calls back, her voice filled with that mixture of authority and care I've come to recognize.

"Please, get me out of this chair. I really hurt," I say, trying to keep the pleading out of my voice, but it's there. I can't help it. Every inch of me is begging to be released.

"You need to be up for fifteen minutes," she replies firmly. "Then I'll put you back in bed. It's important for your recovery."

Fifteen minutes. It feels like a lifetime. I try to shift my focus, to look at anything other than the plain white walls that have become my prison, to focus on something new, anything to distract me. The window nearby reveals a harsh, bright landscape outside, blindingly white—snow, spread across the ground, the rooftops, everywhere. The sight of it sends a chill down my spine, though not because of the cold. I've never liked snow.

I don't know why I hate it so much, but the thought of it, so stark and lifeless, unsettles me. I don't want to look at it, but it's all I can see. The snow seems endless, mirroring how trapped I feel in this chair, in this room. And still, the minutes drag on.

They put me in this chair two, sometimes three times a day. Each time, the pain flares up so intensely that I almost forget why they say I need to do this. They tell me it's to help with circulation, to keep my muscles from wasting away. But all it does is make me feel more broken, more defeated.

Then, one day, Nurse Amy comes in with a new look on her face. She tells me gently, "They were planning to fix your pelvic bone, Mark, but you got very sick right before the surgery. They had to cancel it."

I try to absorb this. They were going to fix my pelvis? Maybe if they had done it, I wouldn't be feeling this constant pain. I wouldn't be strapped into this chair day after day. But it didn't happen, and there's no saying when or if they'll try again.

A new heaviness settles in my chest. The realization that I was so close to some kind of relief, only to have it slip away, leaves me feeling even more trapped, like I'll be stuck in this cycle forever.

Over time, my body starts to respond to all the treatments, and slowly, the doctors start to see me as stable. Nurse Amy tells me that I'll soon be moving out of the ICU and into a regular room. It's supposed to be good news, a sign of progress. But all I can think about is how much I just want to go home.

The regular room is quieter, less frantic than the ICU, but it feels no different. I still have the same unyielding pain, the same restless hours of staring at the ceiling, waiting for something—anything—to change.

Days pass, but I lose track of time. The days blend into nights, and the only thing I know for sure is that I want to be anywhere but here.

And then, just when I thought I couldn't take another minute of it, the doctors gave me a small piece of hope.

"We're transferring you to a hospital closer to your home for rehabilitation," they said.

It wasn't what I wanted to hear, but it was something. "Why not home?" I asked, the desperation clear in my voice.

The doctor looked at me with sympathy, his voice gentle but firm.

"Well, you're going to have to relearn a lot to be able to take care of yourself the best you can," he explained. "So, when you're ready, that hospital can send you home."

His words were a blur, the specifics lost on me. All I heard, all I focused on, was the faint glimmer of hope:

"You are zero weight-bearing. Do not even try to use your legs." It was another rule, another limitation, and I was already planning to ignore it.

At the rehab center, things went from bad to worse. I got sick again, ending up back in St. Louis. A few days later, a physical therapist came into my room with a set of long bars, his face serious as he explained what we were going to do. He set the bars up in front of my bed and told me to get into the wheelchair.

"I can't do that," I said, panic rising.

"I have a broken neck, and I can't use my legs. The doctor told me not to even try."

But the therapist was insistent, his determination unwavering.

"Your doctor sent me to do therapy with you, and we're going to get you up on your feet. Don't worry; I'll make sure you don't fall."

Reluctantly, I let him move me into the chair and wheel me to the bars. With his help, I managed to stand, my legs trembling with the effort. Just as I got to my feet, a nurse walked in, her face paling as she saw what was happening. Moments later, four nurses and a doctor came rushing into the room, their faces a mixture of horror and anger.

"Did you not look at his chart?" the doctor yelled at the therapist; his voice filled with disbelief.

"Get out now!"

The nurses carefully got me back into bed, their hands gentle but firm as they repositioned me. The doctor sighed, shaking his head in frustration.

"We're sending you back to rehab tomorrow if everything is still doing well," he said, his voice tired.

"Back to rehab again," I muttered, feeling a crushing sense of resignation.

But this time, I was only there for a week before the doctor told me they couldn't keep me any longer. "You're just making a bigger hospital bill," he explained, his tone matter-of-fact.

"But before you go home, you need to learn how to safely transfer in and out of your wheelchair."

It was almost too much to believe. Tomorrow, I would be going home. The thought was surreal, almost too overwhelming to grasp. But it was real. I was going home.

But even as I tried to focus on the positives, the reality of my situation hung over me like a dark cloud.

My journey wasn't over. In many ways, it had only just begun. The road ahead was uncertain, filled with challenges I couldn't even begin to imagine. But for now, I was home, surrounded by the people I loved. And for the first time in what felt like an eternity, that was enough.

It was now April, and as I crossed the threshold of my house, a flood of emotions crashed over me. I realized, with a start, that today was Good Friday. In two days, it would be Easter Sunday, and I would be at church. I would be home.

9

oma Cronicles

In the depths of my coma, time ceased to have any meaning. It became an abstract, slippery thing, impossible to grasp or define, as if I were floating in a vast ocean with no sense of direction or scale. For six to eight weeks—at least, that's what they told me later—I drifted in a strange, dark realm, my consciousness reduced to a fragile thread that seemed barely tethered to the world. Days, nights, hours—none of it mattered. Everything blurred together in that endless void, and I existed in a place where the passage of time felt both infinite and irrelevant.

I floated in the darkness, but it wasn't an empty space. No, the void that surrounded me was heavy, thick with an oppressive weight that pressed down on me, yet it was strangely familiar, like a blanket wrapping around my mind. It was a realm without sound, without form—a shadowy expanse where my thoughts were my only companions. And those thoughts were fragmented, splintered like shattered glass scattered across a floor. They would rise and fall, forming brief, blurry images and half-remembered scenes before vanishing again into the abyss.

There were moments—fleeting, almost imperceptible—when I became aware of something beyond the darkness. It was like being underwater, and occasionally, far above, I would see a glimmer of light filtering down, a reminder that another world existed beyond this shadowy sea I was trapped in. Those glimmers were faint and rare, like distant stars on a cloudy night, but they were enough to remind me that I was still connected, still somehow part of something larger than the void.

The memories I have from this time are mine alone—not crafted by stories others shared with me later, not shaped by the accounts of doctors, nurses, or my loved ones. These memories are raw, unfiltered, and entirely my own. They're not clear, not like the neatly packaged moments of a story, but rather flashes, sensations, a patchwork of feelings and fleeting images that form an incoherent yet deeply personal narrative.

I remember grasping at the edges of reality, trying to piece together who I was, where I was, and what had happened. It was as if I were trying to solve a puzzle, but every time I reached for a piece, it would slip through my fingers, dissolving back into the shadows. **Was I alive? Was I dead?** I couldn't tell. All I knew was that I was somewhere in between, caught in a liminal space where the boundaries between life and death seemed blurred beyond recognition.

There were moments when the darkness felt like a comfort, a place where I could hide from the pain and confusion of the real world. It cradled me, offering a kind of strange solace, as if it were saying, "Stay here. You don't need to worry about anything. You don't need to fight." And for a time, I wanted to stay. I wanted to surrender to that comforting nothingness, to let go and drift forever in that weightless, timeless expanse.

But there were also times when the darkness felt like a torment, a prison I was desperate to escape from. The silence was suffocating, the isolation unbearable. It felt as though I were screaming into the void, but no sound would come out. I wanted to break free, to claw my way back to the surface, to the light, to life—but I didn't know how. I didn't even know if it was possible.

Yet through it all, there was hope. A fragile, flickering hope, like a single candle in the middle of a storm. It wasn't always there. Some days, or moments—if you could even call them that—it seemed to vanish completely, swallowed up by the darkness. But then it would return, faint but unmistakable, whispering to me that this wasn't the end.

There was one memory—one that stands out more clearly than the others—where I felt the presence of something, or someone, outside of myself. It was as if a hand had reached through the darkness and brushed against my soul, just for a moment. I can't explain it, but I knew, deep in my heart, that I wasn't alone. That there were people, forces, fighting for me, praying for me, willing me to come back. I couldn't see them, couldn't hear them, but I felt them. And in that moment, I knew I had to keep fighting, no matter how impossible it seemed.

As I navigated this shadowy expanse, I clung to that hope. I clung to the belief that somewhere, beyond the darkness, beyond the confusion, there was light. There was life. There was a future waiting for me. And though my memories from that time are jumbled, disjointed, and often don't make sense, they are a testament to my perseverance.

It's strange to think about now, looking back. To know that while I was lying there, unconscious to the world, my mind was still fighting, still grasping for a way out, still trying to make sense of the chaos. These recollections, though scrambled and incomplete, are a part of me. They are my story, my truth, and though I may never fully understand what happened to me during those weeks, I know that I survived. I made it through the darkness.

And in sharing this, I hope you find some meaning in my experience. I hope it serves as a reminder that even in the deepest, darkest places, there is still a spark of light. Even when the world feels like it's falling apart, there is still hope. And sometimes, that's enough to keep you going. Martin

10

A Brief Note to My Readers

You might wonder why I didn't start at the beginning, but the answer is simple: this is a true story, told from my point of view. At the time these events were unfolding, I had no idea what was happening to me or why. To me, it was a puzzle—a confusing, terrifying experience that I'm still working to piece together. And now, you're reading along as I attempt to make sense of it all.

Imagine being trapped in a world where time has no meaning, where days and nights blur into an endless stretch of darkness. This was my reality. I was aware, yet unaware; conscious, yet unable to interact with the world around me. It was as if I was floating in a void, grasping at fragments of memories and sensations, trying to hold on to the essence of who I was.

Throughout this journey, I clung to the slivers of hope and memory, resisting the pull of despair. I believed that even in the darkest night, there is a promise of dawn. This belief kept me going, kept me fighting, even when the odds seemed insurmountable.

As you read this memoir, you'll find that it's not just a recounting of events, but a testament to the human spirit's resilience. It's about the power of hope, the strength of love, and the unyielding will to survive. I hope that my story will inspire you, give you strength in your own battles, and remind you that even in the darkest times, there is always a glimmer of light.

Please understand that, in my mind, everything was a jumbled puzzle I was struggling to piece back together. Friends and family might recall details and moments that I didn't include in these pages. This is my attempt to make sense of it all, to share my journey with you, and to find meaning in the chaos.